The Meaning of Being Human

The Meaning of
Being Human

NORMAN PITTENGER

The Pilgrim Press
New York

Library of Congress Cataloging in Publication Data

Pittenger, W. Norman (William Norman), 1905-
  The meaning of being human.
  1. Conduct of life. 2. Life. 3. Meaning
(Philosophy)   I. Title.
BJ1581.2.P57   128   81–15762
ISBN 0–8298–0489–7

The Pilgrim Press, 132 West 31 Street, New York, NY 10001

Contents

Preface

S OME YEARS AGO there was a song from a musical play that was heard continually wherever popular music was sung or played, and that is still heard from time to time today. It was "Ole Man River"; and in the song were the words, "I'm tired of living and scared of dying." They expressed the feelings of a lonely character in the play; but they also expressed how a large number of men and women felt and still feel about their own lives.

Henry David Thoreau, the nineteenth-century American naturalist, once spoke in much the same way. He said that every man feels now and again what he called a "sense of quiet desperation" about his existence. And the Danish writer Sören Kierkegaard, now so much read in intellectual circles, characterized this existence by the word *angst,* or anxiety. Quite recently, too, Paul Tillich (known to many through his writings and lectures) penetrated beneath the superficial cheerfulness of contemporary life and in his Terry Lectures at Yale University spoke of the "sense of meaninglessness" which is hidden deep in many people. His lectures were entitled *The Courage to Be* since they stressed the need for courage if one hopes to live meaningfully in the world as we know it so well today.

Some have said that the characteristic mark of younger people today is optimism. We are told that they have accepted the fact that we must live "under the threat of the bomb" and that they acknowledge the "inhumanity of man to man," about which Wordsworth wrote. Yet at the same time they are said to look at things with considerable hope. This may be the case; but my own contacts with university undergraduates and others would indicate that such hope is, so to say, "against hope." They, too, with their sincere concern for saving the planet from ruination by human carelessness, their often radical political and social views, and their genuine desire for racial understanding, have a basic uncertainty about whether human existence is meaningful or whether their activity (and sometimes their retreat to inwardness) is merely a busyness to avoid facing the question squarely.

Naturally I do not know how those who pick up this book look at themselves and at their lives. But for myself I can say that after much more than three quarters of a century of life, I still feel the need to find some meaning in existence, if such can be found. If there is none, the advice of an ancient Greek writer would seem best: "End it as soon as possible." Why should one not do this, if life is only "a tale, told by an idiot, full of sound and fury, signifying nothing"?

Yet the fact that I do *not* want to end it, nor do most of the others whom I know, has some significance. It indicates that we are prepared to go on living; it also indicates that in some sense or other we feel life has a worth and value. It might be put even more strongly, I think. The willingness to go on living demonstrates, in a subtle fashion, not only that some meaning may be found but that some meaning *has been* found. We cannot express this in any precise way; yet human life, simply in and of itself, has a quality about it which makes it *good*. It gives us sorrow and anguish; it also brings us happiness and joy. There is a worthwhileness in living which we take more or less for granted. This I believe to be right; and in this book I shall try to say why.

For the title of a semiautobiographical book the French novelist André Maurois chose an old classical adage, "Never call a man happy until he is dead." As one read the book, however, one was struck by the amount of satisfaction Maurois appeared to have got from his life—despite the many tragic incidents he recounted. To at least one reader it seemed that Maurois must have been one of those people who cannot be happy unless they speak gloomily; they enjoy having been miserable, even if at the moment the misery was appalling to them. But that attitude in itself tells us something. It shows that deep down in many people, below their level of conscious awareness, a sense of life's value persists.

In this book I can speak only for myself. But my purpose is to help others see, as the title says, "the meaning of being human." I address the book to ordinary men and women like myself; and I speak out of personal experience of "what it feels like to be human." Not that I intend to speak autobiographically, save for the final pages. But this book tells how one man, who has lived through all but five years of the present century, can still believe that human existence is worthwhile. I send the book out, then, in the hope that it may have put in a simple way the common but usually unexpressed conviction of most of us: that this world is not a bad place to be in and that living in it can be a good, even a joyful, experience.

The Meaning of Being Human

1

Can Human Life Have a Meaning?

C AN HUMAN LIFE have a meaning? During the Middle Ages the great scholar Thomas Aquinas asked this question in beginning one of his discussions: "Does God exist?" And he answered the question with the words, "It does not look like it." That was an honest way to begin his discussion. Of course, he went on to attempt a demonstration that, although "it does not look like it," it is yet true that God does exist. But the point is the honesty and realism of his starting place.

At the top of this page I have put the question, "Can human life have a meaning?" And, like Aquinas in respect to God, the immediate, off-the-cuff answer may very well be, "It doesn't look like it." But maybe, like Aquinas, we can discover that being human can and does have a meaning, despite that which seems to argue against it. But certainly there is a great deal which makes life's meaning doubtful; and I must speak briefly about some of these negative suggestions.

Any sensitive person looking around these days, and perhaps at any time at all, sees a great many things which would seem to argue against there being a significance in human existence. There are wars and rumors of wars. There is an enormous amount of physical, mental, and emotional suffering. There is injustice and cruelty wherever we turn. Worst of all, there are the broken dreams and disappointed hopes with which we have tried to console ourselves. To have lived, not just to have existed like a vegetable with some slight degree of consciousness, is to have known times when there seems to be absolutely no sense in life. Each of us has experienced suffering and grief and bereavement, frustration and futility; each of us knows what it is like to be without friends, work, a home, or the deep fulfillment that can bring us joy—or, if we have not experienced these ourselves, we can readily put ourselves in the place of those who have. Human life can be a very sad story indeed. We must not, we dare not, minimize the loss and tragedy that are there.

Most of us, however, seem to feel that we want to go on with living. The suicide rate is not sufficiently high to suggest that the majority of men and women find the whole business too painful and too frustrating to endure. Furthermore, a case might be made for the position that the reason that bad or wrong or evil things make such a devastating impression upon us, is that we usually find our existence tolerably good. This good provides a sort of backdrop against which the other things stand out clearly and in bold relief. Probably most of us would agree that a carefully prepared balance sheet would show a reasonably large sum in black figures and a somewhat smaller sum in red ones.

This would suggest that the genuinely realistic person is not necessarily the complete pessimist. Of course some have assumed that such must be the case. But is it? A cheerful optimist of the rosy type, who refuses to look evil in the face, is certainly unrealistic and there is nothing to be said in his or her favor. But perhaps true realism is found in the man or woman who, while recognizing perfectly well that life is no bed of roses (and even if it were, roses have thorns that can be very annoying), also feels that, in the main, life is worth living. So he or she is prepared to get on with it, troubled about what is wrong yet finding occasions for happiness and joy and sensing that, somehow or other, it is good to be alive.

So being human *can* have a meaning. But what then *is* that meaning?

Let us begin by considering ordinary human experience as we all know it. Since we are talking about human life, this is the natural place to start.

One obvious point can be made at once. *Part* of the meaning of being human is just the fact of living. This is not to talk in circles: what I am suggesting is that in the business of going on with life, doing what comes next, fulfilling responsibilities as they arise, continuing with our job, finding our happiness where we can find it, sharing others' pain and knowing our own, we gradually discover a certain genuine satisfaction. There are the terrible moments, not least those of boredom, when there seems nothing to fascinate us. But after a day spent at work—provided the work is not the sort that is utterly destructive of personal integrity—we have a feeling that something has been accomplished, even if it has not been anything which would make a splash on the front page of tomorrow's newspaper.

This is not silly compensation. We are not like the child who was asked why he was beating his head against a wall and replied, "Because it feels so good when I stop." No, not that. For any job which is in the least worth doing, from selling shoes to singing songs, brings some sense of achievement. At the very least we can say to ourselves, "Well, I *did* sell that pair of shoes," or, "I *did* sing that song and the audience did not pelt me with rotten eggs."

This is putting it at a fairly low level. We can phrase it more elegantly if we say something like this: "The meaning of human life is to be found in realizing, making real, what I have it in me to be." That way of putting it brings out a very important truth which most of us understand but which we do not often consciously think about: that everybody does have potentialities that ought to be, and to some degree can be, realized. There is more in a man or woman than meets the eye. There are depths and heights which others do not see or understand. Everybody has *some* potentialities, even if they may not seem to amount to much at first glance. A boy knows he has the potentiality of becoming a man; a girl knows she has the potentiality of becoming a woman; a child starting school has the potentiality of learning to read and write. A man or woman in love has the potentiality of becoming a sharer in life with another person. There is more to us and in us than what we now appear to be, whether this "more" turns out to be for our good or for our ill. We ought never to forget this, easy as it is to do so in moments of depression or loneliness or despair.

The notion that a man or a woman is a "finished article," about whom we may speak as if he or she were a specimen to be put in a museum and labeled "A Man" or "A Woman," is one of the most mistaken and unfortunate ideas that ever entered into our ways of thinking. No human being is a finished product in the sense that a page once printed is just there or that some artifact once made is just there. From our own experience of what it feels like to be human, as well as from our observation of others, we know that we are *becoming something;* we have not already arrived at our supposed terminus. What are we becoming? Here the answer is very simple indeed: *Human beings are becoming human.* This ties in with what was just said about our potentiality. We have in us the potentiality of becoming men and women—not monkeys, nor angels, but *men and women.* Every one of us is on the move, either toward making more real our potential humanness, or toward making it less real. At our best there is a forward look; as the Victorian poet Robert Browning once put it, "Man never is / But wholly hopes to be." He was right. None of us *is*, exactly as and how he or she appears at this or that moment. Each of us "hopes to be," facing toward the realized existence which may be ours, yet constantly forced to make choices or decisions that will be effective for or against that realization.

What has just been said indicates another fact about our human life. If we know ourselves to be on the move, then we must also see that in us there is an interior drive which impels us forward on our way. To be human at all means to be *becoming human;* and there is something in each of us that attracts us toward our goal or (to change the image) pushes us on our road toward it.

Modern psychologists often talk about what they call "the dynamic nature of human personality." They are saying in learned language and on the basis of careful observation exactly what we have just suggested. They recognize that human nature is not static but thrusts forward toward future realizations of possibilities that are present in the material of which we are made. This thrust they often describe as toward increasing integration of everything in human nature, so that a "full man" or a "full woman" may emerge. In the language used above, our realization is simply becoming that which a human being has in her or him to be. This is the purpose or intention of being human at all.

Once this fact is grasped, we can begin to understand the restlessness or disquietude that is part of our experience. Sometimes this is vividly known; sometimes it is hardly present on the surface of our consciousness. It all depends on how we may happen to feel at a particular moment. Of course, most of us find it agreeable enough to "stay put" in the place where we are—but not for too long a time. Sooner or later we get restless: we feel disquietude where we are. We want to move, to go somewhere else. A parable of this restlessness is seen in people who seem to have no particular objective in life toward which they wish to go, yet who are constantly on the move. If they happen to be rich and have sufficient funds to pay their way, they may begin traveling: they board a ship or an airplane or a train; they visit this place and that. They are trying to satisfy this dynamic urge to be on the move; they are restless if they are too long in any one place; they get "bored," as they say, and they want to relieve their boredom. Physical movement of this sort is hardly likely to provide the satisfaction they desire. But such people illustrate that quality of the human spirit that is looking for fulfillment and is trying to move toward it.

All of us feel the need to travel, but not necessarily in a physical sense. There is our urge to be "getting somewhere." I believe that this urge is an obvious way in which the dynamic aspect of human existence expresses itself. "Much have I traveled in the realms of gold," says John Keats in a famous poem. Well, most of us cannot do just that; nor did Keats himself. But in our desires and yearnings we sense the need to fulfill, or make real, all that we might be. Even if we cannot express ourselves very clearly about it, we know what it is to want, perhaps to want desperately, to become our real selves. To achieve *that* would indeed be to find ourselves in a "realm of gold."

Psychologists tell us that human beings have a drive toward integration, which is the patterning of our lives in a desirable and satisfying way, having its center in some aim or goal. And our own insistence has been on such an aim or goal as the fulfillment of our human potentialities. We want to be "whole" people and to know abundant life as a consequence of this wholeness. Nobody is satisfied if he or she has the feeling that he or she is a partial or truncated person. Nobody is satisfied if he or she senses, rightly or wrongly, repressions or frustrations that deny wholeness by preventing movement directed toward genuine fulfillment.

In this connection, we may note that a reason for the protest of many young people in our own day is the feeling that conventional society refuses them this chance to move forward toward their desired wholeness. They may be right or wrong about this. The fact is, however, that a considerable number of them think that this society is set against such fulfillment—perhaps by repressive attitudes toward bodily expression, by intellectual "steamroller" tactics in education, or by insisting on acceptance of social patterns that (to these young people) are calculated to make genuine growth impossible. I believe that they are seeking earnestly, often violently, for human wholeness or integration, so that everything in them may come to fruition. Perhaps they are naive about this; but older people should try to understand them, rather than attack them or dismiss them almost contemptuously.

None of us can avoid the thrust toward desired fulfillment in wholeness. If we did, we should simply curl up and die. The fact that we do not curl up and die is a sign that deep down inside us, somehow and somewhere, we are inevitably on the move, drawn toward realizing our human potentialities, pushed toward this goal by circumstance, frustrated time and time again, yet once in a while feeling that we are indeed on the right path. This is the way human beings *do* exist.

Probably most of us do not work it out or analyze it in this fashion. Certainly we make serious mistakes, deciding wrongly about how to use our powers. This fact of wrong decisions indicates that there is a need for discovering the *right* way to become human. Part of the meaning of being human, then, is a capacity for choosing among possibilities offered to us. Here we have to keep our eyes open and use our heads. This is natural to us, yet it must be cultivated. It is human to be alert to chances offered for right and sound growth; or, as we may phrase it, to be awake to opportunities and challenges that show us which direction is best for us to follow.

Animals have eyes and they use them. They may have heads, too, and use them. But their capacity for such use is less rationally ordered than ours is. Human beings have a distinctively human way of keeping their eyes open and using their heads. Some of us do not have perfect twenty-twenty vision, of course; some of us do not have richly endowed heads (or brains, for that is what we are talking about here). But such as they are, we can use them both, more or less reasonably and with greater or less imaginative understanding. If we refuse to do this, we are less than human. And we can do what I have styled "cultivate" them, beginning where we are and as we are.

G.K. Chesterton once remarked that it would be silly to tell a crocodile, "Come on now, be a *crocodile*!" After all, the beast is doing that to the fullest extent of its "crocodility." However, it makes sense to say to a woman or man, "Come on now, be *human*!" When we say that, we mean: "Start to realize what you have it in you to be. Make decisions directed toward that end. Begin now and keep on in that way. That is what you are here for." This makes sense because it speaks to something in us that knows perfectly well, however we may hide it from time to time, that this *is* what we are here for. We are meant to move toward self-realization, integration, and wholeness, making the decisions that help us along the road. In other words, one aspect of the meaning of being human is found in our choosing—by decisions freely taken, so far as this is possible under given circumstances—to follow the direction that best promises what we seek: to become genuinely human. A moral dimension is built into life.

Many think that talk about morality necessarily implies arbitrarily imposed laws, some set of commandments handed down from on high. These must be obeyed, lest we suffer punishment or damnation. No doubt morality has often been presented that way, but there is no necessity that it should be. In any event, such a way of understanding it does not seem very human. Talk about a moral code that is forced on us with little regard for our human possibilities, succeeds in making nonsense of our deepest moral sense; and it is that deep moral sense which matters most. I am talking about the profound awareness that one is moral only when one is free. Decisions which are imposed upon us, so that we have not the slightest chance to make a negative response, are lacking in moral quality. You can only act morally when you have some opportunity to say yes or no, and when you are ready to accept the consequences of your decision. So a moral sense is something deeply rooted in human nature itself. The *moral dimension* in human living is nothing more nor less than human living *in its choosing or deciding according to its best lights*—although, of course, each of us can profit from listening to the wisdom of our ancestors as this has been embodied in so-called laws and commandments. Often enough, that wisdom is of very great importance and we do well to attend to it and follow it. But there are times when "New occasions teach new duties, / Time makes ancient good uncouth." The right decision for me, here and now, must be a decision that is possible for me to make; somehow it must be within my reach, so that I can meaningfully accept or reject the given possibility. Otherwise we are talking about coercion and not about morality at all.

In its essence, this moral dimension cannot be given precise statement. But we can now see that one part of the meaning of being human is the making of free decisions, so far as this is open to us—and along with the decisions, the readiness to accept responsibility for the consequences of our decisions. The decisions must be possible for us and relevant to our situation. And there is something more:

right decisions affect not only ourselves but other people.

Later in this book I will have much to say about the social quality of being human. For the moment, let us simply recognize that a central element in the meaning of being human is relationship with others of our species. John Donne wrote, "No man is an island, entire of itself." Insofar as we are human, we are knit together, bound up together, part of the great human community. Of course it is possible to think, in an abstract sort of way, about a baby growing up entirely alone, unrelated to others, and existing for years in isolation and insulation from the human race. But would that baby become genuinely human? It seems to me that she or he would become a slightly more intelligent animal—and even then intelligence would be limited, since we grow mentally as well as emotionally by contact with other people.

In view of this "sociality" of being human, which is the other side of the "personality" of being human, our decisions must take others into account. The human moral dimension is not an individualistic affair; it has social overtones, social bearing, and social results. This is why another aspect of the meaning of human existence is deciding in such a way that we promote the right fulfillment of others, as well as our own fulfillment.

If each of us did only what seemed "right in his own eyes," regardless of others near or far, the result would be anarchy. It would be a chaotic condition, very likely to end in appalling conflict between and among us. To avoid such anarchy, social structures or patterns have been developed in human history. These are not ideal, by any means; they are in need of constant revision. Yet they do avert the danger of sheer anarchy let loose on the world. Senseless conformity, without question or criticism, to such structures can be deadening; but an anarchic condition would produce endless war.

The Greek philosopher Aristotle begins one of his books

by saying, "Man is a social animal." For "social," he used the word *polis*, the Greek word for city: a Greek knew human social relationships only in terms of the city where he or she dwelt. What Aristotle did was to move from the discussion in the first part of his writing on morality (called the *Nicomachean Ethics*), where he talked more about strictly personal matters, to the insistence in a later part (called the *Politics*, by an unhappy translation of *polis*) that we do and must live together. For him and for all of us the meaning of being human is not only in free decisions, but in our responsibility in those decisions for a deepening relationship with others.

A deepening relationship with others—yes, this is part of the meaning. But to be effective, such a relationship must be based upon more than the mere fact of a common humanity that all share. There has to be some common loyalty, too, in which all may share. A cause to which we are devoted, a person to whom we are loyal, a purpose which we accept in common, an agreed motivation —without something of this sort it is impossible to establish real *community*. Notice that word community; it is derived from Latin and its root meaning is common agreement. Such agreement, sometimes vividly felt but often only dimly in the background, gives us what we need to live for, maybe even to die for. Loyalty like this unites us as persons-in-the-making in a community-in-the-making.

For some of us this became very clear during World War II. It has often been pointed out that never before in their history were the people of Britain so united as during those terrible years. The unity was not merely a matter of sharing in deprivation, suffering, and peril. Its true basis was an association in loyalty to all that Britain meant to them and in the common determination to defend that meaning. Homeland, culture, family affection, freedom, and the other things about which Churchill spoke during those years, found their symbol in "king and country." The people who lived in the United Kingdom were genuinely *united*. They were standing together for what Churchill often called the cause of truth and justice and decency in the world. What was true then and there is in its degree true always and everywhere in the enterprise of human living.

An important consequence of common loyalty is deliverance from too narrow a concern for individual interests. When we forget ourselves and center our attention on whatever it may be that has commanded our supreme allegiance, we discover that, far from losing our identity, we have been enriched, become more truly human, and sense a growing integration of our personality and a genuine fulfillment. Decisions that must be made have in view a more enduring satisfaction, precisely because that satisfaction can be shared with others. Immediately attractive or appealing choices are tested by whether they contribute to the common good, for each person wishes to play his or her proper part in the task laid upon all.

The wisest men and women of our race have always spoken in this vein. They have told us that it is in losing ourselves that we find ourselves. This sounds paradoxical, perhaps absurd; yet experience bears it out. Join with others; recognize that you are one with your fellows; accept them, as you hope they will accept you, as partners in the work that is to be done in service of this commanding cause or person or principle, and life seems better and more fulfilling. So we can say that still another aspect of the meaning of being human is just this participation in community. We have to live *beside* our fellows. It is our privilege, and gives sense to our existence, if we also live *with them*. Somehow human life is structured that way; and if we go against this structure we are impoverished in our innermost selves. It is much better to go along with the grain of the universe, so to say.

The business of sharing with others brings us to the last point in this chapter. The point is very simple yet it needs to be made. Let me put it starkly, in one short sentence, and then make some comments. The clue to the meaning of being human is in the word *love*.

The word can suggest many different things and later we shall have to consider it in greater detail. For the moment it is enough to say that the love about which I am speaking is a relationship of mutuality, of giving-and-receiving, of openness to others. The people whom the human race has most honored have known and said this. Gautama Buddha in India, Confucius in China, and Jesus in Palestine, to name a few, have taught, and in different ways have expressed in their lives, this very simple truth.

Just before writing these pages I was leafing through an anthology of sayings by those men I have just cited and by many others, too, including Ikhnaton in ancient Egypt, the Hindu seers, Iranian prophets, the great Hebrew prophets, and many others. The idea appeared time and time again: it is love that gives life its savor and makes it meaningful. Surely all these wise people cannot have been wrong; their witness is too unanimous for us to think that. These great ones were moving toward, some of them were explicitly affirming, this strange yet compelling truth. For us in the Western world, the climax is seen in Jesus of Nazareth. And not only in his teaching but in the very fabric of his life as remembered and set down in writing in the four Gospels. But he does not stand alone here; if he is the culmination of this profound movement of thought, many others have glimpsed the truth and sought to teach and live it.

Love is what fulfills because it is what unites. I spoke of the "grain of the universe" a few paragraphs above. The people whom I have mentioned were convinced, despite the great differences in their backgrounds, cultures, and personal qualities, that *love* is the grain of the universe.

They knew all about evil in the world, the wrongs in human existence, and the wickedness that so often seems to prevail. Yet they did not waver in their assertion. Could their insight be sound and penetrating? I believe that it is.

But ordinary men and women sense the same thing. If we turn to popular songs—"You're Nobody Till Somebody Loves You"—and sayings—"All the world loves a lover" —this assertion is made time and time again. Some of us who are older will recall how Victor Herbert had a song telling us how "all the world" is seeking the love which (as he put it) is "the secret" of human existence. For myself, some words from an English poet of Elizabethan times speak home: "Not where I breathe, but where I love, I live." The man who said that was Robert South-well, who had a difficult existence in his own day as a Roman Catholic recusant suspected of treachery to queen and realm. Yet he said this and he meant what he said. When lovers tell the beloved, "I love you," they are really saying that deep inside they are aware that the love wherewith they love is greater than themselves; it is the way things *go*—and it is the path to genuine fulfillment of human potentiality. For then we are doing more than breathing (important as that is if life is to go on), we are *living*, as Southwell said.

It is at the human level that this is recognized, of course. Whatever more is to be suggested follows from that human experience. For us humans it *is* love that makes the world go round. Maybe it is love which makes everything go on, the love of which Dante wrote in incomparable Italian, *L'amore che muove il sole e le altre stelle:* "the love that moves the sun and the other stars." About that we shall say something at the end of this book.

Anybody who has come to love another, anyone who has been ready to receive love from another, will know whereof I speak here. In a mysterious fashion, love is able to bring us to fulfillment, to satisfy our drive or thrust toward realizing our potentialities, to put us on the right path when we have gone astray, to make us truly human. So I end this chapter by repeating what can never really be expressed verbally but only in concrete acts: the meaning of being human is nothing other, nothing less, and nothing more, than love.

2

How Can We Know It?

I F, AS WE HAVE ARGUED, love is the meaning of being human, how can we come to know it to be so? The question has already been partially answered in the preceding chapter but a fuller discussion will be helpful. The briefest way of putting the matter is to say that we can come to know love as the meaning of our human existence in only one way: by our own experience of loving and of being loved. But obviously such a short explanation must be expanded.

First, however, there is one point that needs attention. After reading what I have said so far, someone may remark, "All that is very well. It reflects a real part of life and says something true about the meaning of that part. But what about pain and suffering in love? What about the agony that so often accompanies this love you are talking about?"

That is an entirely proper comment. We dare not overlook the facts to which it points. In our experience of love, which gives its meaning to our being human, suffering, pain, and agony are most certainly present. This is what a Spanish proverb expresses when it says, "To make love is to declare one's sorrow." That is no Latin exaggeration, although the phrasing may suggest this. It is a plain statement of something known to every lover, every lover-in-the-making, whoever he or she is. To love is not sentimentality, neither is it merely a pleasurable sensation. *Love hurts,* whether it is we who love or we who are loved.

Nobody would doubt that in loving there is often a pleasant or agreeable emotional content. There is also an element of sentiment; but that is different from sentimentality, which is simply luxuriating in our nice feelings. Feelings are part of loving, of course. We love with our whole selves and our feeling-tones are part of our selfhood. It is also true that, in one sense, love is very simple. No lover constantly has a growing sense of its many complicated details in his or her relationship. Although there are plenty of problems and questions, the relationship itself in its fullness is not complicated. But because deep and true love is a giving of self to another self who in turn gives, and because love is positive, outward-going, and concerned, it has about it a sacrificial quality. Is it not the case that to give, wholly and entirely and from one's very depths, is never easy or painless?

Furthermore, when we are caring for, concerned about, and ready to surrender all of ourselves to another, we inevitably share with the other his or her cares and concerns. We share in his or her joys, but we also share in his or her pain, suffering, and sadness. Joy in love is not the negation of this sharing but its victorious result—and it is always a joy that is tinged with some degree of anguish.

I am confident that any reader of this book who has known truly deep love and has let this love have its way with her or him, will readily understand what I am saying. Our own experience of loving verifies it. If, for example, we feel at the moment that we have lost (somehow or other) the one we loved, we will yet agree with the familiar words that "it is better to have loved and lost,

---

19

than never to have loved at all." Our love may seem to have taken wings, to have come to an end—perhaps through death or through some shattering experience of separation or rejection—but we know that once it was glory and wonder for us. We will say that we were really *living* when we had that loving relationship. Now, without it, we are only "partly living," in T.S. Eliot's words. But the very fact that we now have this sense of only "partly living" is an indication that once we were *fully* living. Otherwise we could not make the judgment about *this* moment in our experience. And if we are realistic and honest, we cannot deny that during the time when we knew this all-mastering love we also knew agony. The very word passion has a double meaning: it signifies both the overwhelming emotion of love-in-act and also the experience of anguish. Would not we welcome back the agony, if we could also have the love? Here is the strange and paradoxical quality of love. It may not often be expressed in precise words, maybe not even consciously understood, but many people who on the surface seem unimaginative realize deep down inside that genuine love is not cheap nor sentimental but a total giving of self which inevitably brings pain to him or her who loves and is loved.

What is more, if loving is the way in which we best realize our human potentialities and move toward wholeness or integration through our free decisions to accept or reject given possibilities presented to us, then some degree of suffering is necessarily involved. When I make a decision I am inevitably saying no in order that I may say yes. That is, not all the given possibilities can be accepted; some must be cut off (the word decision comes from the Latin term for cutting off). To make the *right* choice is to refuse the *wrong* ones. To decide for this, not that, is to cut off *that* so that *this* may be affirmed positively. Human life in this respect resembles a necessary surgical operation in which we may be obliged to suffer the cutting out of *this* part in order to secure the proper functioning of the *total* organism. One thing is sacrificed in order to ensure something believed to be better. All this can and does *hurt*.

Some years ago there was a novel with the unusual title *What Makes Sammy Run*. My point here is that what makes each one of us run—genuinely live with our dynamic thrust forward and our shared experience with others—is the double experience of joy in pain, triumph in suffering, delight through anguish. Each pair is a unity; together they provide a meaning which redeems the human enterprise from cheap triviality and from comic absurdity.

Let us now return to the question asked at the beginning of this chapter: How *can* we know that love is life's meaning? My suggested answer was: "We can know it by actually loving." The answer is given *solvitur ambulando,* as the old Latin tag puts it: it is proved in the doing.

Often enough, as we all know, some problem that concerns us is solved by our simply "living with it." We come to know what is the case, by trying it out and seeing whether it can demonstrate its truth to us, one way or another. To say this is not to fall back on a shoddy sort of practicality, wherein truth is only the immediate workability of some idea. What I am suggesting *is* practical, to be sure; it *is* pragmatic. Yet I should stress that what I have in mind is long-range and fruitful practicality, not just a "quickie." The living with the question is not for a few minutes only; it is a matter of taking time. That ought to be expected. Anything worthwhile, anything really worth doing, inevitably takes time. The quick answer, the immediate and thoughtless response, the proof given by snapping one's fingers: in most instances these are likely to prove fallacious. They are too easy; and life is not an easy affair, as we all know. When a boy and girl have "fallen in love," as we say, there is usually a longer or shorter period of courtship, during which they give themselves time to see whether they are really in love, really ready to embark together on life's way. I believe that this is how it must be with us, as we seek to prove to ourselves that life's meaning is love. Robert Frost said somewhere that we look at the world as a problem to be solved and we begin our effort to solve it, only to find that we are not solving a problem but are embraced in the arms of a lover. The world not only loves a lover; it also appears to *want* lovers and to make sense of their loving. Dare we say that something deep down in things is here speaking and acting through our ordinary human experience of urgently yearning to give ourselves and to receive from others, or another, the returning gift of self? Evidently Robert Frost thought so.

The only way to know that love is the meaning of being human is by taking risks. Human life is largely a matter of taking risks, anyway. We might prefer a world in which everything was neatly settled, but as it happens we do not live in such a world. Simply to be alive at all is a risky matter, even if we do not spend much time thinking about it. There is risk when a baby emerges from the warmth and security of the mother's womb. There is risk when an adolescent takes upon himself or herself the responsibility of entering mature adulthood. There is risk in any and every decision we make, even when to all intents and purposes it appears that we are "bound to win." Life consists in risking ourselves as well as in risking what we possess. My *life* is always at risk. This is not a very comforting thought but it happens to correspond with reality and we had better accept the fact—if we do not, we are looking for trouble, for disappointment, for disillusion, and ultimately for sheer despair. Most of us, however, see the point. We may not talk about it nor put it into so many words, yet we are prepared to take risks because we feel that there is no other way toward the goal that we want to reach.

What this means is that being human entails an attitude of faith. I am not speaking here about *religious* faith in any narrow sense: I mean only what a Harvard professor of a few generations ago, Kirsopp Lake, was getting at when he said, "Faith is not belief in spite of evidence, but life in scorn of consequence." This saying suggests some important avenues of thought.

There is something which has been called "animal faith." This is simply the business of going on as a living, sentient, conscious creature (conscious, that is, at the *human* level—although below that level, consciousness is doubtless without such self-awareness)—prepared to take the risk of living at all. Every animate creature has something like that; in humans it is at a more or less conscious level. If an animate creature did not have such a capacity, it would not be animate; it would be like a vegetable, existing serenely in a vegetative state. On the higher levels of life, faith becomes more than "animal"; it becomes conscious, something of which we are aware. And finally in human beings, with their developed rationality and their ability to know themselves, it becomes a specific entrustment of their lives, involving thought and will and desire.

Human faith is an act of the total person. But as Lake said, it is not to be understood as "belief in spite of evidence." Plenty of evidence is around to make the act of faith look absurd. This is true not only of the creeds to which many religious groups ask their members to subscribe; it is also true of the appearance of things as they are, which do not always seem to point toward meaning or value in being human. But this is not the point, since faith is "life in scorn of consequence." It is a total life-attitude, a totally engaging life-act. Perhaps the word commitment will best serve to describe what we are talking about. Or, we may prefer to follow the modern existentialists and speak of "engagement," in which the person in faith gives himself or herself to and engages with some cause or person, and does this "in scorn of consequences."

When I truly love, I give myself in that way. I commit myself, I engage myself, with all that I have and all that I am. I surrender myself totally to that which, or, better, to him or her whom, I love. "I am his" because I have been brought to grasp the astounding and shattering truth that "he is mine." I engage myself with the other, so that each of us "belongs" to the other who is loved. Perhaps this is why the word engagement is commonly used when we wish to say that a boy and girl, man and woman, lover and beloved, intend to establish a relationship openly and publicly acknowedged, a relationship that even now is partially existent in its concrete reality.

Without commitment of self to self, there is no genuine love. What we find in that case is something much more superficial: physical attraction, emotional satisfaction, or perhaps nothing but lust in the pejorative sense of mere urge for physical gratification without enduring relationship. I say "nothing but lust" because I want to make it clear that lust, as such, is a genuine element in true love. Lust in itself means the urgent desire to be united with another, physically as well as in other ways. The desire is entirely good and sound. But, as we all know, lust can be dissociated from love in such a way that it becomes the wish to *possess* another, most often physically, but without concern for that other as a total human being. Thus we need to be careful lest we fall into the mistake of denying the importance and goodness of desire, on the one hand, or of thinking that desire means only the urge to own another person, on the other. When Jean-Paul Sartre speaks of human sexual relations as a battle in which each of the partners tries to conquer and possess the other, he shows how badly he has understood the basic significance of sexuality. It is entirely human and entirely right to desire to unite oneself with another person, thus sharing the whole self (including the body) with the other: it is appallingly inhuman and wrong to think that this can be possession or simply the gratification of the senses, without further consequences in the total life. (More must be said about the matter in a later chapter.)

One reason that all the world loves a lover is that there is something touchingly beautiful when two people, perhaps especially two young people in all the eagerness and energy of youth, engage themselves to and with each other. We may even be moved to tears, for it is always deeply moving to see people who are truly in love. And the very phrase "in love" needs to be taken with the utmost seriousness. For to be in love is a condition in which we find ourselves, in two possible senses of the phrase. First we discover that this *is the situation*. It was not manufactured by us; it was given to us. If it had been manufactured, made up or worked out by us, it would be subject to the changes and chances of life and to an unplanned but inevitable obsolescence. Lovers know that this is not the case, which is why they can say with the marriage service that they will and must love one another "in sickness and in health," as well as "for better or worse, for richer or poorer." Second, we find *ourselves* for what we truly are, when we are in love. We find ourselves as we hitherto have not been able to do. We plumb depths of our human existence, we recognize potentialities of which we were unaware, we see ways in which we may become our true human selves. We see these in ourselves; we see these in the one we love. Thus we discover ourselves and others in our common goal of whole and integrated personalities, realizing or making actual the stuff which we have in us and which can be used to make us truly human.

We spoke earlier of the feeling of those in love that their love is greater than either of them. We need now to go on to say that in the experience of human loving there is a deep, usually unexpressed, awareness that the relationship somehow is so *real* that it cannot be analyzed away in terms of feeling-tones, emotions, physical reactions, or anything else. The love is a personal reality into which the lovers enter and in which they share.

It is true that physiologists can speak of the chemistry of love; but they are wrong if they think it is only a matter of human glandular reaction. It is also true that psychologists can speak of emotional attraction or satisfaction of the libido; but they also are wrong if they think love is that and nothing more. Those who know love from experience cannot, or ought not, deny the facts about which these experts are speaking. They will insist, however, that while chemistry and libido are very much part of the picture, they are by no means the whole picture. The error comes when the physiologist or the psychologist presumes to use the word only to preface his statement. Indeed that little word, like "merely," is always dangerous, since it may lead us to commit what might be called the "nothing-but" fallacy. There is all the difference in the world between saying that such and such is necessarily to be taken into account and saying that such and such is the whole story. A person is an animal, but he or she is not *only* or *merely* an animal. If that were so, the word human would never have been invented to indicate a particular kind of animal that is *also* more than an animal. This nothing-but fallacy was prevalent for a long time in certain scientific circles and it has had a wide and baleful influence elsewhere. What we need—and happily what more and more scientists and others are trying to give us—is a total or organic picture of ourselves and of everything else. In that sort of picture the various pieces will fit together and their proper relationship will be understood. So it is here: glands, yes, and emotional libidinal satisfaction, yes, but also something more. Love is bigger, more inclusive, more significant than any of its several psychological or physiological aspects. Perhaps we may say simply that the lover is aware of being in love *and* of becoming more and more one who is *in* love.

I am not playing with words just to be clever. I am trying very hard to get at a genuine reality of human experience. My appeal is simply to that experience and my protest is against whatever would deny its richness and its indicative value, by which I mean its pointing toward an enduring importance in how things actually go in our being human. It is too bad that sophisticated experts do not always pay sufficient attention to what ordinary people say about what they feel and know. Professor C.D. Broad of Cambridge University once remarked that there are "some theories so absurd that only a very clever person could have thought them up." The "nothing-but" people are the victims of that mistake; they are so learned, so expert, so taken up with their particular field of study, that they have no time to bother about "what every man and woman knows." This is, of course, absurd.

Thus we come back to the question of how we can know that love is the central clue to the meaning of being human. I have said that it is by actually living it out—that is, by *loving,* by *being* in love, by the experience of being *in* love. We prove it by the experience of it, getting our question answered as we proceed to act in a natural and ordinary way as people who can and do learn to love. We will not get it by abstracting ourselves from experience in order to devise clever theories. The answer cannot be stated in the neat and precise definitions that we hanker for; it can only be found when men and women who are lovers discover for themselves that it gives meaning to their existence. They delight in it even while they also suffer from what another Spanish proverb calls "the sorrows of love."

Human lovers know that they are being fulfilled most wonderfully by their mutuality, their giving-and-receiving, their life together. They know that they are becoming more truly themselves, with the discovery of potentialities that they were not aware of possessing, and with a capacity to realize these potentialities that before would have seemed utterly incredible. They feel a wholeness in their existence that both satisfies them and gives them joy. Of course they do not spend their time talking about all this; they are far too busy in their loving, far too urgent to express their love, far too delighted to receive love, and far too impelled to act lovingly to others around them. Only in a retrospective or meditative mood will they think much about these things—and then, only occasionally. But that does not matter. In their delight and satisfaction they sense that there is no need constantly to talk of or to theorize about what is happening to them. As we shall see, this applies not only to the more intense kind of love with its obvious and specific sexual overtones, but also to friendships at a very deep level. In these latter love is also present. And in both sexual love and friendship it is often better to be silent and to enjoy. When Thomas Carlyle and Ralph Waldo Emerson met for the first time and realized the depth of their friendship, they sat together without saying a word. They simply enjoyed being with each other and there was no need to chatter.

One thing is perfectly clear. We cannot learn in our own experience that love is the meaning of being human unless we are open and ready to love *and to receive love*. I stress the last phrase because there is a mistaken idea that love is nothing but the giving of self. This is another example of what I have called the nothing-but fallacy. Love *is* giving; but it is also receiving—and often it is more difficult to receive than to give. In any event, the person who is twisted in upon or twisted around himself or herself—Luther had a fine Latin phrase for this: *incurva-*

tum in se, "curved in upon oneself"—and not open to love or to be loved, will never find love's meaning nor will his or her human existence amount to much. By a false centering upon self, such a person will have lost the chance of discovering the deep truth about love.

The person who is selfish in that sense *cannot* know what it means to be human. And why? Because that person fondly thinks that one can "make oneself," whereas nobody can do that. We depend upon others; and human meaning is not manufactured out of the whole cloth by us ourselves, but is given as a gift, shared with others and enriched in the very sharing. People who are falsely centered in self are cursed with an existence that is basically meaningless, however successful they may appear. Sooner or later the time will come when they will see how futile it has been for them to win whatever success they may have achieved, for they will have lost the one thing needful. They may have gained the world, but they have lost their own soul. That is a saying attributed to Jesus of Nazareth; its truth is established every day. What is more, such people not only lose their chance to discover what it means to be human, but they can also be highly offensive to those with whom they have to do. Thus the situation is made unpleasant for everybody.

In other books I have noted that the word spinster has often been applied to women, but in my opinion it should be equally (if not much more so) applicable to men. A "spinster" is frequently not just an unmarried man or woman, but an embittered, warped, self-regarding, self-righteous, ultra-puritanical person whose false feeling of goodness leads to condescension toward, if not condemnation of, others. Not every woman who is unmarried, nor every man for that matter, is of this type. We may be grateful for that. There are many unmarried people who are open to love, ready to be loved, although their way of loving and being loved is not sexually intense. Sadly, there are also plenty of married men and women who, for some reason, have let themselves become spinsterish.

Usually this happens because of disappointment in such love as they have already experienced. Yet this need not result in a warping of personality. The suffering, pain, and anguish that somehow accompanies our human loving can be used differently; it can deepen sensitivity and it can teach us about ourselves and about others. Above all, it can show us that in human life we cannot have everything we want. This is tied in with what I have said earlier about decisions, about cutting off, and about the deep places of our existence, where we must always be alone. The poet Matthew Arnold once wrote of the "unplumbed, salt, estranging sea" that necessarily separates us from those with whom we are in most intimate relationship. I can never become somebody else. In a profound sense, that is the joy in love, as well as its anguish. For love is a *relationship*, not a loss of identity. Part of its enormous delight is the guarantee of freshness, the element of surprise, which sheer identity would make impossible.

In love there is respect for the other—even reverence. In some of the older marriage services, the word worship was used, as when the man said to the woman whom he was espousing that "with his body" he "worshipped her." That may seem somewhat odd to us. Yet is it not the case that to worship, with the body as well as with all the rest of oneself, is to respect and reverence another for what he or she is on the way to becoming? Reverence here has nothing to do initially with what I may actually be able to give or do, although this will follow; it is a matter of seeing the beloved simply *as* the beloved.

Last of all, in the experience of love we become aware of the beauty of the world. That may seem an extraordinary thing to say. Yet consider the words of one who loved another very deeply, and who told me this: "It is as if everything around me is suffused with glory—grass and trees and flowers, sky and stars, the other people too." What hitherto had seemed drab and dull, uninteresting and perhaps even ugly, now appeared to him in a new light. He did not deny what he knew to be evil and wrong; yet, in his own words, "the world looks lovely."

Exactly so, for the word lovely can have two meanings, both significant in this connection: "filled with love" and "attractive or winsome." I end this chapter by some comments on this point.

I began this book with a quotation from Thomas Aquinas. He had two other sayings which deserve attention. In one, with splendid Latin brevity, he tells us that "goodness is diffusive of itself" (*bonum diffusivum sui*)—it cannot help but shed itself abroad, radiate out, give. In the other, he speaks of beauty and calls it "the splendor of being." Both of these sayings are relevant here. Love, deeply known and shared, *does* spread itself, radiate, and give; at its best it is utterly unselfish. It showers itself all around; it takes into its embrace everything in the world, save only the evil and the wrong. Even there it can see the good hidden in distortion and wickedness—it will indeed hate the evil but love the misguided, erring, wrong-headed person who does that evil. And then the world is seen to be lovely; it has about it the splendor of being. There is a discernment of a basic harmony in things to which our own growing wholeness responds. Men and women learn that this is so, as the key to the significance of being human, when they risk themselves in love and find that it verifies itself.

3

The Place of Work

WORK—THE VERY WORD calls up to many of us a picture of sheer boredom; meaningless routine; tiresome activity done only to earn enough money so that existence is possible; something that goes on all day and from which at 5 P.M. escape is offered, so that at least there is a chance to "live." Yet, despite this picture—for which perhaps the biblical depiction of work as "the curse of Adam" has some responsibility—not all work, nor work at all times, is so deadly and dull, so lacking in purpose and value. For work can provide not only an escape from the worry and loneliness that so many suffer but also material for the realization of our human possibilities. It can even be a source of genuine happiness for those who engage in it. It can be an opportunity to develop toward genuine wholeness. And it can be these without our denying that much of what we must do during our working hours *is* boring, repetitive, mere routine, and perhaps unpleasant.

There are some types of work that are so monotonous as to be almost soul-destroying. There are others that seem degrading and loathsome. One way in which this might be overcome would be by an ordering of human society in such a fashion that types of work which were really unpleasant or disagreeable should be spaced out and exceptionally well rewarded in terms of wages and benefits. This would not remove the problem entirely; but it would help. Furthermore, technological progress seems to be providing ways in which at least some of these tasks can be done in some other fashion. But this is not a book about social reconstruction, economic problems, social justice, and the like, although, like everybody else, I have my own opinions on such matters. All I can hope to do here is to speak of work itself, in the widest sense of the word, and make some suggestions about how it contributes to our becoming the men and women we are meant to be.

One thing is immediately apparent—indeed so obvious that it hardly needs saying. Work of some kind is a help to us in avoiding the sort of idleness which is even more destructive of personality than the most unpleasant kind of job. The man or woman who literally has "nothing to do" is all too likely to be the man or woman who becomes nothing at all. The "idle rich" are an object lesson here. Some of them have no way of using their time except in pursuit of immediate pleasure; theirs is a pointless and inane existence. We see this if we happen to spend a few days at a resort much frequented by people of this sort. Their sole concern is to "amuse themselves," and the sort of amusement which they seek, unlike the play and recreation which we shall consider in the next chapter, produces nothing but emptiness. Anyone who is busy in pursuit of empty frivolity presents a depressing spectacle. The observer sees that energy is exerted with no return, save futility and boredom—energy that might well have produced fruitful and shared good. The ennui and tedium of a life spent in doing nothing offers a picture that is truly horrible. What is more, all genuine meaning for being human is ruled out from the start.

But there are rich people who do not need to work in order to live, but yet have found things to occupy their time and energy. As I write I think of an acquaintance who, by worldly standards, would be considered very well off. He could lead a life that would require no work at all. Yet this man has interested himself in a variety of causes which have constructive social value. He is one of the most energetic persons I have known. He stands in striking contrast to some of his friends who spend all their time going from one place to another in order to escape from themselves and the emptiness of their lives. He does not need to engage in a frantic pursuit of superficial amusement in order to keep his mind off the ghastly vacuity that many of these friends must feel in the dark hours of the night.

Most of us are not in this situation; we are not wealthy enough to avoid work and we need to have a job in order to support ourselves in the sheer business of living. For us, work is a necessity; we cannot escape it even if we should like to do so. What can we say, then, about this situation?

In even the most interesting work there are bound to be periods when we carry on simply because it is our responsibility to do so, if we hope to retain our job. One of our problems is how to accept the tedious monotony which inevitably seems to accompany work of any kind, however exciting it may appear on the surface. This is as true of an artist as it is of a worker at a desk, a teacher, or a man or woman in a factory. There is no escape. We have to learn to accept the dull moments and use them in a constructive and positive way for the development of our total selves toward the great goal of becoming ever more fully human.

From my own experience I have come to believe that

there is an approach that will help us here. I speak from more than fifty years as a teacher, a kind of work that may appear to be much less tedious than many others. But anyone who has been a teacher knows that the hours can sometimes drag terribly. If you try to explain a point to students who are not very responsive; if you spend long periods assisting them in preparation of essays or dissertations; if you must prepare carefully for your lecture or classes—you do not find it all exciting or thrilling. The approach of which I speak can be stated very simply, although in actual practice it is not at all so simple. I am talking of training oneself in the attitude, or developing in oneself the frame of mind, that puts emphasis on the *main* ends in view. This is a question of one's perspective. How does one look at the job? What purpose can it be thought to serve? In what way may it benefit others? Can the worker and his or her fellows somehow secure from it a richer, better, fuller realization of potentialities?

It would be dishonest to pretend that every job can readily be appraised in that way. Many kinds of work seem to serve little or no obvious purpose—at least no purpose that can be appreciated as good or valuable. Much work does not appear to benefit oneself or other people; it does not look as if it helps the fulfillment that is our ultimate goal. Yet it is possible to discern *some* kind of relationship to that goal. The woman who sells cosmetics may find it difficult to see the value of what she is doing. But if another woman is helped to find satisfaction by making herself more attractive, there is something significant in selling the cosmetics. That is a trivial illustration, but like many things that appear trivial it has its element of truth. A man who keeps accurate accounts in an office is at least helping to make sure that the business is conducted honestly and with social responsibility. Someone who is engaged in what we unhappily call manual labor very often performs a great public service. The repairman who came recently to my rooms to make an adjustment to the electrical heating apparatus not only showed remarkable expertise in his technical work, but also did something to enable one person to live and work in relative comfort during the cold winter months.

If a job is worth doing at all, some kind of sense can be made of it. What seems surprising is that work that on the surface is sheer monotony can assume a meaning. There is an old and hackneyed story about a man on the assembly line who, when asked what he was doing, did not reply with the obvious answer, "Stamping this piece of plate," but said, "I'm making an automobile." Hackneyed though the story may be, it points toward a very important truth. Such an awareness of value is not going to be in the forefront of consciousness every moment; someone who is at work is usually too busy to give attention to wider purposes and hidden possibilities. But that is true all through life. From a very different sphere we may cite a couple engaged in what we style "making love." In the exalted moments of joy that accompany lovemaking, they will not be thinking about the deeper significance of what is taking place. They will not have vividly in mind that their lovemaking is an expression of total surrender of each to the other, establishing a union where achievement of personal wholeness is made possible. Yet in that lovemaking the pleasurable sensations and the sheer delight in the experience of physical union, dominant at that moment, are contributing to a significance that is central yet unexpressed.

To give another example, I am at this moment working on a book which I hope will be of some interest to its readers. My *main* intention is to help them to come to some understanding of the meaning of being human. I also have a "subintention": the possibility that I may secure some small extra income from its publication and sale. But at the moment of writing, as my fingers busy themselves with putting words down on paper, I am more immediately concerned with this almost mechanical task than with the main intention or even the subintention. My immediate job is to write as clearly as I am able, so that readers may understand what I am saying. Furthermore, because I have decided that a book of this sort must not be too long, each chapter must have a limited number of pages. Therefore I must concern myself with phrasing what I want to say as succinctly as possible, thus making sure that the chapter will not exceed the desired length. There is drudgery here. Yet every now and again, especially as I begin to write in the early morning, I am aware of that main intention and I know perfectly well that this is what the work I am doing is all about. I am also conscious from time to time of my subintention: for if the book is accepted, published, and sold I might receive as royalties some extra money to use for purposes that seem good to me.

There is nothing very subtle in such a description of my work at the moment. There is nothing peculiarly mystical about it. It is quite simply a combination of the notion of a valuable purpose, as I see it, *and* the hard work of doing what I have set myself to do in the best way I can.

Again from my experience as a teacher, an illustration may be given. I am required by my job to spend a good deal of time supervising students in the preparation of doctoral dissertations. If anyone thinks that is easy, let him or her try it! Yet it can have meaning. It is part of the total pattern of my responsibility. Years ago I chose that pattern; I decided that I would be a teacher and when opportunity arose, that I would be a teacher in higher education. I did not then directly elect to spend dreary hours looking at students' outlines or going over their preliminary drafts of a dissertation. Those hours are simply part of my job. Such work is not always tedious, by any means. But when it is, the tedium can be accepted by seeing that the major end or goal is to help others to formulate their ideas precisely and clearly, to show their genuine academic competence, to receive their advanced degree, and to be able to find work that their degree merits. Thus I can become a more complete person by helping others achieve their own goal. I share with them so that they may develop their potentialities and I discover that in this sharing I am myself fulfilled in surprising ways.

These are rather special instances, but the principle that they embody is widely applicable. All I can do here is to ask my readers to consider their own work, whatever it may be, and see if something of what has just been said can be applied in their own case. I feel confident that it can be, although obviously the ways in which this may be done will vary enormously in terms of opportunity, sort of work, and personal factors. Generalizations are helpful, provided they are not used as a steamroller to remove all the distinctions and differences in our experience. My hope is that this particular generalization will prove its validity; my belief is that it is able to do just that.

An old saying has it that "all work and no play makes Jack a dull boy." That is true enough, but it is equally true, if not often said, that "all play and no work makes Jack empty and unfulfilled." Experience surely bears this out. We have spoken of the idle rich; let us be honest enough to see that we who are not rich can fail to recognize the value of sheer work for us. Furthermore, routine is part of work and we are none the worse for it. Routine delivers us from fatuity. A friend once told me that for him routine was a blessed thing because it made it possible to carry on in spite of his momentary emotional states and his wavering sense of pleasure or displeasure in what he was doing. It enabled him to get through the dull spots because he had learned through routine to accept that dullness as part of his job. I think he spoke wisely. So did another friend who remarked that the test of one's conviction that one's work was worthwhile was a willingness to put up with what he styled the "dead moments." He went on to say that those dead moments provided for him an occasion of delight since they were so much part of what he considered a valuable contribution to society. Perhaps he spoke too enthusiastically, but he made a point.

Human life is an alternation between work and play. Part of our being human is in doing our share in the ongoing corporate existence of the human race; another part of it is in what we do for refreshment and recreation. But an alternation requires that both parts be present. That is why work without play makes Jack dull and it is also why play without work makes Jack vapid. I will speak about play in the next chapter; here I need only say that any work that has lasting value includes engaging ourselves with our fellows in the human community, apart from which there can be no real meaning in our being human. Entirely personal meaning is nonsense: all meaning must be *shared* meaning. The ultimate goal for us as persons-in-the-making, and for the human community to which we belong, is the satisfaction that comes from an awareness that whatever we do, be it work or play, has been well-done. I did not say perfectly done. That would be asking too much. I said well-done, by which I mean as well-done as we can make it. We should not forget, however, a comment of G.K. Chesterton: "If a job is worth doing, it is worth doing badly." I presume he intended by this that at least *something* has to be done, however inadequately and imperfectly. Yet the *aim* is a well-done piece of work, for only that can provide us with the satisfaction we so much desire to feel. And here, dedication to the job is all important for us. Most slipshod results come from lack of such dedication. Nor do I mean by dedication anything particularly noble; I mean only what an old craftsman, whom I knew more than half a century ago, was getting at when he said that he always tried to make a table that had been ordered from him as good a table as he could manage. That was real dedication; and that old man was a very simple and ordinary chap, with no pretenses and no claims to extraordinary skill.

We now realize that men and women are psychosomatic creatures: our physical and psychological lives are interdependent. I have already made rather a special point of this in my attempt to portray human nature. Now I can argue for its importance in the matter of our work. If that work is largely physical, it also has its mental and emotional effects; if, however, it is largely mental, it takes its toll of our physical energies. We need to remember this, lest we assume that those whose job is, say, with their hands can never know mental fatigue and those whose day's work is spent sitting at a desk or reading and writing cannot become physically exhausted after many hours of work. But there is something else which should be borne in mind. Because we are body-mind organisms, with strong emotions as well, we need work, of whatever sort, to keep us occupied.

When I am working, concentrating my whole personality on the job at hand, I find that I am less conscious of the aches and pains that can become so unpleasant when I am doing nothing. Perhaps I might even say that my general state of health is better—mentally and physically as well as emotionally—when I am occupied with my work. This is not to suggest that there are not physical ailments which are serious and require attention. Of course there are—and part of our being human should be both an awareness of such ailments and an effort to remedy them. What I am talking about here is the danger of hypochondria, when people spend much of their time fussing about supposed illness or worrying about the state of their health. My suggestion is that when we are busy we do not exaggerate such feelings and anxieties, as we are

---

40

likely to do when we have nothing to engage our full attention. An acquaintance once told me that when he was harassed by worries or felt aches and pains as he grew older, it was his habit to weed the garden. "Then I find the worries and the aches assume their right proportions," he said.

It would be a happy situation if everybody could engage only in the kind of work that had great interest or that had been personally chosen. Alas, this is not how things are for most people. I have been fortunate in the chance to choose my own work; but in this respect I suppose I am one of the privileged few. Most people must work in order to exist at all, to support their families, and to have the ordinary necessities of life. They cannot decide for the job that appeals to them; they must take what is available. Thus for a large part of each day they are working at tasks that they do not always find very appealing. There can be no doubt about this; although once more we can say that our increasingly technological society is helping us here. Nonetheless, much of the easy talk in schools, colleges, and even universities about choosing a vocation can seem somewhat nonsensical. In a way, our job chooses us, rather than the other way around.

Yet a great deal will depend on how we define that word vocation. Sometimes it is used as a kind of omnibus word to cover any and every type of work that a man or woman may do. But the more basic meaning of the word, I suggest, is different. The word vocation is a Latin derivative and signifies calling. Now what *is* our calling as human beings? In the most profound sense it is to realize ourselves, to develop our potentialities, so that we may become what we are meant to be. The vocation or calling of every man or woman, without exception, is to become a fully realized human being. Work must contribute to that end; it is not only desirable but essential that somehow it should do just this. But the basic calling is to move toward wholeness or integration, to make our decisions and choose our path, in such a way that the end product will be a life in which we are gradually becoming the kind of lovers about whom I have spoken.

Whatever our job may be, and whether we have chosen it or have been obliged to take it because of circumstances beyond our control, that job can be done in a way which will help us in fulfilling this vocation to true human existence. My contention is that adopting this attitude toward our work can give that work a certain justification and establish its value. For example, the man who looks at his work as a simple nuisance is hardly likely to find much happiness in life. He is like the playboy who refuses to share in the common lot and devotes all his time and effort to being amused. Obviously, there is nothing wrong with play or amusement; it is only when these are made the *whole* of life that they become dangerous and can lead in the long run to vacuity or emptiness. It is part of human existence to be a sharer in the network of relationships, which includes a contribution to society through work that has to be done. We do not live in the Garden of Eden, where presumably work was unnecessary. We live in a world that is arranged so that everyone is responsible for doing a share of the work to keep society going.

There is a prayer in one of the denominational service books that speaks of our doing the work that is ours "in beauty, in goodness, and in truth." That may seem a rather idealistic statement yet it has truth in it. I can decide that whatever work I do will be undertaken and performed with the intention of bringing some good to others. I can try to place that work in a pattern which will be harmonious with my total human existence; hence the job will be done "in beauty." And I can seek to do my job "in truth," with honesty and integrity, without cheating or making false pretenses. In these ways I can find at the very least a minimum of satisfaction and at the same time

I can discover that my work is one of the ways in which my true vocation to grow in human fulfillment is realized.

There comes the time of retirement for most of us. We can no longer continue in the job that has been ours; we are put on pension or farmed out. That does not mean that the need to engage in some sort of work is over and done with. But now the work is much more of our own choosing. This is why it is so useful to have a hobby, begun in earlier years and in our retirement able to provide us with something to do. I knew one man who had been hard working during his whole life. He was obliged to retire, at an age slightly beyond the normal one. But, alas, he had nothing to do. He had time and money and he thought that he would pass his remaining years amusing himself. But the unfortunate thing was that he had no real interests, no hobby, nothing which could engage his attention. His search for amusement became rather ridiculous and at the end he resembled the small child in a very progressive school who was heard to say, "I don't *want* to do what I want to do!" Perhaps he wanted to do something that would be useful to himself and to others, but there was nothing to help him. He had not prepared himself for such a thing by having a hobby or by developing some genuine interest in his earlier days. He moped, he fussed, he worried. And within a short time he died. The doctors said that he had died because he seemed "to take no interest in life." It was a tragedy and it need not have happened as it did. He would have died, of course, sooner or later; but he would have died happy and without making himself and others miserable by his inability to find contentment in retirement. I thought at the time, as I think now, that this man's failure is a lesson to us all.

It may be platitudinous to say that an aimless life is hardly human, or that one of the ways in which we can be delivered from such aimlessness is by having a job and doing it as well as we can. Like so many platitudes, these statements are simple truth. Yet we should also recognize that our work is not the *whole* of our life. Being human includes doing a job but it includes a great deal more.

"Variety is the spice of life." We have mentioned the alternation between work and play that helps to keep us fresh and alert and alive. There are other aspects of life that do the same. For nobody is *just* a worker and nothing else. Look at John Jones. He is an accountant in a large business firm. But he is also a husband and a father. He is a member of a trade union. He belongs to a fraternal organization. He likes to watch the television and listen to the radio. He goes to the movies and occasionally to the theater. He is associated with a religious body and attends church services. He is a great many things in addition to his obvious classification as an accountant in a business office. Each of these other things makes its distinctive contribution to his basic vocation to become a full man. Above all, his relationship with his wife and children, with his friends and neighbors, develops in him his capacity to become a genuine lover, in ways appropriate to each type of contact.

John Jones is realizing himself, hence finding meaning in being human, in his own distinctive way. He is not Henry Brown and his manner of becoming himself will not be the one suitable for Henry Brown. Each of us has an inalienable selfhood. There is no stereotype which will exactly fit every human being. When we say "humankind" we are not talking about an abstract humanity, but about *this* and *that* man and woman. Each of us has both the right and the duty to be uniquely himself or herself. Here again, but in a different sense, variety is the spice of life—or, as we often say, it takes all sorts to make the world. We have every reason to be glad that this is so. How ghastly it would be if we were all the same, nothing more than identical entities stamped out by some mechanical process.

Having said this, however, we should also remember that we are social by nature; we live beside, with, and in our fellows, and cannot become truly human in some supposedly pleasant isolation from others. Certainly the meaning of our own personal humanity is known to us only as we do what is given us to do, either by the choices we have made or the obligations imposed upon us. But this meaning will be truly effective for us only as we realize that we are not alone, as if we were the *only* human being in the world. We are tied to others, whether we like it or not; we are dependent upon them, even if we might wish it were otherwise. We can find our meaning —and with it our measure of human happiness—when we live with others in a generous and open relationship. This does not require us to be cheaply tolerant or softly sentimental but does demand that we shall permit ourselves to be in a situation of giving-and-receiving. True fulfillment of selfhood is with others and for others, by virtue of our sharing together in the human lot. This is why love, which is exactly such sharing, is the clue both to the meaning of each of us as we grow in our work toward fulfillment, and to the wider meaning of human society as a whole.

4

Amusement and Play

THE DISTINGUISHED DUTCH historian Huizinga has written a book with the title *Homo Ludens,* "Man the Player." And medieval thinkers included among the defining characteristics of human nature the capacity to laugh; man was said to be *animal risibilis,* "the laughing animal." Perhaps they would have agreed with the familiar saying quoted in the preceding chapter, "All work and no play makes Jack a dull boy." In fact they would probably have gone farther and said that anyone without the capacity to play and to laugh is to that degree less than fully human.

Surely no one doubts that play of an apparently purposeless (and certainly nonprofitable) sort—along with laughter, joking, "seeing the funny side," and the like—is a good and valuable part of human life. It pays no dividends but it gives us enjoyment. A man or woman who cannot take time off from work and engage in some type of play is altogether too serious. He or she lacks the redeeming quality of levity, which at the right time and place relieves human existence from monotony, overly intensive concentration, and worry about earning one's living. I should contend that play is more than this, however. It is part of the meaning of being human.

In this chapter I want to speak seriously about the importance of not being too serious, for one of the most important things about being human is to be able to take time not to be serious. The man or woman who is overly earnest is a bore.

There have not been very many learned books written on play and fun; and those which have been written seem rather dull. But here we have no need to engage in a learned inquiry into the subject. The matter can be put fairly simply.

When we speak about play we intend to indicate the kinds of activity in which human beings engage when they are not concerned to earn money or pursue learning or discover truth. We are talking about something which is not duty or responsibility but is sheer fun. People play because they get pleasure from doing so; and this is right and good. The man who is playing golf as an amateur will naturally wish to reduce the number of drives and putts required to get a ball from a tee into a hole on a green. If he is really playing golf for fun he will not care very much whether he or one of his partners has the lowest score. Naturally he will enjoy winning; but the heavens will not fall if he loses. The professional golfer is different, of course, but here I am not speaking about those who make sport or amusement their work: I am thinking of the genuine amateur. It is interesting that the word amateur comes from the French and means someone who engages in an activity for the love of it. "The game's the thing"; and we like it that way.

So also with other kinds of amusement. Naturally some of them feature professionals who entertain the spectators or the audience—for these professionals, what they do is their way of earning a living. The rest of us, however, are "having a good time." We are enjoying a period of relaxation and getting pleasure from recreation. Such activity is good and contributes greatly to the significance we find in life. This is not full-time activity, but part-time; and much of its charm comes from the recognition that this is the case. We need the variety which play and amusement bring us.

Sometimes, for example, we can indulge in some fanciful flight from the hard and harsh world of everyday experience. We can forget the struggle for financial returns and economic security. Provided we return to our work refreshed and renewed, we have done no wrong. This is not the wrong kind of escapism, but a realistic appraisal of the sort of beings we are. Sometimes, too, we may enjoy a drama that deals with some serious theme. We may be edified, instructed, or deeply moved by it. But what makes it entertainment is that it is somewhat removed from the exigencies of our own workaday life.

Everyone knows the refreshment that comes when someone makes a good joke or utters a witticism. Once again, this is because it is one step removed from the humdrum way in which much of life seems to pass. To see things in an unusual way or from a different angle, or to put thought and word together in some unexpected juxtaposition, gives a new slant on human existence. Sometimes it helps us to see that we ourselves are funny people. In one of my books I have quoted the French thinker Henri Bergson, who in *Le Rire* gives an example of rather blatant humor. He speaks of a man slipping on a banana peel and in consequence finding himself precipitated onto the street. Bergson asks why most people find this a humorous situation. His answer is that we are seeing the poor man forced to do accidentally what he would never think of doing in his normal routine. But there are more sophisticated kinds of humor. There is a juggling with words, a slight distortion in the meaning of a sentence, a change in phrase from the commonplace and accepted.

These bring a smile to the face; perhaps they cause us to laugh out loud.

I do not claim that I have given a neat definition of play, amusement, humor, and the like. Of course not. For part of the delight we find in these derives from the plain truth that we *cannot* define what is going on. Their charm is in the purposelessness, the unexpectedness, the refusal to fit into a pattern of highly serious definition. But two words that I used earlier provide us with some help in seeing how play, amusement, and humor are aspects of the meaning of being human. The words are *relaxation* and *recreation*. Both are essential in our movement toward fulfillment as humans. I will speak first about relaxation.

Most of us are obliged to concentrate on our work for a large portion of each day. We focus attention on its details. Inevitably there is a certain tenseness here. We may get "all keyed up," as the phrase goes. If we do not, it is probably because we have so accustomed ourselves through practice to this concentration that we now take it in our stride. Even so, the tenseness is there, deep down in us. For most of us, however, it is pretty much on the surface. We tend, perhaps unfairly, to consider as frivolous a companion who does not show some of this concern. Certainly we feel that a person who does not realize that the work at hand is to be a contribution to the human community as well as a way to personal growth, is not sufficiently earnest (in the *good* sense of that word).

Precisely because in the doing of our work we are likely to be tense or concentrated, we need to "unwind." We need the moments when the tension is relaxed and when concentration may be stopped for a time. If an elastic band is continually stretched to its limit, it will snap. Something of that sort is true of us. If we are tense every minute, in concentration the whole day, our ability to do a good piece of work will be lessened. We will become dull and brittle persons under the threat of a "breakdown." We need relief, not only so that we may work better but also so that we may be more human. Play, amusement, and humor make this possible. They provide the essential relaxation of concentrated effort; and they also provide occasions for us to sit back and enjoy life.

And why should we not enjoy life? Only a puritanical approach would suggest that enjoyment is bad. Such an approach reminds one of George Santayana's definition of a fanatic: "a man who redoubles his effort when he has forgotten his aim." For the aim of life, as I have often urged, is simply to be human in the deepest sense of the word. Effort which is so intensified that it makes us tense can remove from our awareness this ultimate goal. It is possible—but tragic—for a human being to become nothing but a machine for work, resembling the characters in Karl Kopek's frightening play of the years between the wars. These characters were "robots," mechanical toys and nothing more.

I have always felt that even the extreme Puritans recognized somehow the need for sheer enjoyment in human life; it is too bad that in the classical statement of that need they put it off to heaven. The Westminster Catechism begins with a question about "the chief end of man" and answers by saying that it is "to glorify God and enjoy him for ever." Naturally that answer has a specifically religious import when it speaks of glorifying God but it *does* speak of enjoyment, in heaven at least. It may be the case, indeed, that the religious dimension in human experience has an important significance. I believe that it does, as my final chapter will show. But when religion is reduced to moral earnestness and that alone, it can lead to a narrowing of personality and become a disagreeable thing for others. Nonetheless, it is good that the Westminster divines of the seventeenth century were not above mentioning enjoyment.

Relaxation brings enjoyment in relieving us from tension. And enjoyment gives a right proportion to human life. Much the same can be said about the other word which I have suggested: recreation, or refreshment. I now turn to that aspect of play, amusement, and humor, to see how it fits in with the movement toward the goal of human fulfillment.

The person who can find no time for play, amusement, and humor is likely to become intense, bored, perhaps overwrought. That person will also become *stale*. Someone like this may become miserable and feel that he or she is not accepted by others, is perhaps disliked by them, is not welcome in their company. All that poor person can do is think and talk about work, in which others are probably not very interested. The feeling of rejection, whether based on fact or not, compounds one's own inner insecurity. What is needed then is recreation and refreshment, to see one's own existence and everything else from a different angle. We all need this from time to time. We must "get out of ourselves" and have the grace to learn that we and our affairs are not so important as we often like to think. In that way we can also learn humility, for humility is basically a sense of humor about ourselves. The men and women who cannot see themselves and their activities with a certain humor are likely to be so centered in themselves that they are unable to enter into the lives of other people. They suppose themselves to be content perhaps, but their inner insecurity denies them *real* contentment.

To say all this is not to deny for a moment the disquietude that, as we have seen, is characteristic of our being human. Such disquietude is of a different order from what I am now discussing. Genuinely human disquietude is a sense of unfulfillment or failure to realize potentiality: it is a sign of our recognition that we have more in us than we have yet expressed or made real for ourselves. This is good. But my point in respect to humorless people is that they have *not* seen themselves as they really are. They have not accepted their present condition as the precondition for further advance. They have fashioned for themselves an image of one who is hard pressed, overworked, indispensable to the world. Thus they have failed to understand their own dependence on others. They need the refreshment that is gained by learning a certain lightness of touch, a humor that will relieve or redeem the heaviness of their burden of responsibility, real or assumed, and enable them to grasp the fact that everything does not depend on them and on them alone.

Our next chapter will deal with human beings as lovers, with a special emphasis on the pervasive sexual quality of all loving. But right here it is useful to say that in such love there is always an element of play. Lovemaking, both in the broader sense of being in mutual relationship with others and in the narrower sense of sexual contact, is indeed a serious matter for us; but it is not to be engaged in as if it were *work*. To speak of lovemaking as play may seem shocking to some people; but it is much more shocking to deny this. For if love is not play it is either a professional affair, so to say, or a matter of mechanics. In the former case, love and lovemaking are reduced to a kind of prostitution. In the latter, the delight and wonder is lost in a zealous concern for technique. This is often suggested by the books which supposedly instruct people in "how to make love." They succeed in turning what is essentially a free and spontaneous relationship into a series of rules to be followed; and the result may be that the partners are so much concerned about keeping the rules or obeying the directions that the sheer fun of love, including sexual love, has no chance to emerge. Love and lovemaking are an art; and like all art, they include a large element of play. There is no need to dwell on this point, since lovers know very well that what brings them joy is "doing what comes naturally" in a spontaneous expression of the desire to share life and in the passion present when two people are truly in love. It is important, nonetheless, to make clear that, in at least one sense, love has the quality of play and amusement, maybe even of humor.

Still another point of considerable significance is the value of "economic waste." The phrase was used by the famous American economist Thorstein Veblen in his valuable protest against the reduction of all human effort to profitable work. As he said, there is much in life which has no economic value and which produces no measurable economic returns. Visiting an art museum, listening to a symphony, playing a game, reading a book, talking with friends, making love, even going to church are examples of activities that, for the most part, fall into this category of economic waste. Of course, the professional critics of art, music, drama, literature, or sports would not think of their work as wasteful since thereby they earn their living. But for the rest of us, simple enjoyment or pleasure, sometimes accompanied by the pain felt when a painting or play or piece of music or book speaks to deep places in our souls, is what we are looking for. We do not expect the kind of returns which might be entered into an account book showing debits and credits. There is no way in which the value of these pleasures can be expressed in terms of the laws of economics. The delight is there; pleasure is experienced; satisfaction is known—and that is enough.

It is right and good that things should be that way. For each of us is much more than an economic creature. We are a whole living being whose purpose in life is to become more and more human. We find our enrichment and fulfillment not so much by listing our profits and losses as by the satisfaction felt when we are indeed becoming ourselves. Tragically, this side of human experience has often been forgotten, even by those who considered it valuable. Yet increasingly we are discovering that leisure, recreation, opportunity for relaxation and refreshment, are of the highest importance. As human society faces a growing use of technological substitutes for human labor, more time is being freed for something other than work. We are told by experts that because of this "cybernetic revolution," most of the necessary labor will soon be accomplished with only a few hours each day required of human agents. These experts wonder what then will be done with the remainder of our time.

Their question is valid, but I should prefer to phrase the matter in another way. Some of the experts, alas, talk of using leisure time as if it were a commodity. They, too, are victims of the economic fallacy against which Veblen protested. I suggest that we spend more of our time in considering not how such leisure time is to be spent, but rather how it is to be enjoyed. To talk of "using" our time is altogether too serious a way of speaking, necessary as it may be when social planners are at work. It is always worth remembering that there is absolutely nothing wrong with enjoyment nor with the sort of activity, whatever it is, that does not involve *work* in the usual sense of that word. What we need to learn for ourselves, and to help others understand, is how we can best enjoy those moments when we are not engaged in the serious business of earning a living or doing our daily job.

Obviously, there are some kinds of play or amusement that are damaging to the proper development of human life in community. There are some kinds of humor that are cruel or lack decent human consideration. These can have a devastating effect. But for the most part, play is just play, amusement just amusement, and humor just humor. They are for their own sake and they need no utilitarian reason for existing. These things are good in themselves and we ought to accept them as such.

54

The same is true of another aspect of human experience that is closely related to this side of life. I am thinking of wonder, reverence, delight, sheer rapture, and awe. Some or all of these may be awakened in us by the contemplation of natural beauty seen in mountains, ocean, sky, or stars. They may be awakened when we know ourselves in the presence of true greatness or goodness in another human. They may be aroused in moments of aesthetic experience or in the religious view of the world. In whatever way they come about, through whatever agency they emerge in us, there is nothing utilitarian about them. They, too, are beyond the debit-credit account. Anybody who tries to use them for profit will probably lose them altogether. The poet Wordsworth in a familiar poem tells us that "his heart with rapture thrills / And dances with the daffodils" seen one day in the countryside. Here was delight and joy, tinged with reverence and awe at the beauty of nature; and the response was *to dance,* not to make an economic accounting.

The contemplation of beauty, greatness, goodness, wherever found, is in a profound sense a "play-full" experience. It has its serious side, of course, for (as Wordsworth also said) "thoughts that lie too deep for tears" can be aroused by such contemplation. Certainly Vergil was right in speaking of *lacrimae rerum,* "the tears that things arouse." Often enough the wonder and awe or delight is so very profound that even tears cannot express our emotion. Or we may be brought to dance, as Wordsworth was—and that would not be surprising, since tears and laughter are perhaps not too far apart. Both are functions of our emotional response to other people and to the world we share with them. But neither of these emotional responses is related to the account-book side of human experience. Their value is not economic but totally personal.

I conclude this chapter by turning to the importance of the aesthetic element in the proper fulfillment of our human personality.

There is a common misunderstanding of the word aesthetic. It is taken to have to do only with what is beautiful or at worst pretty. An aesthetic person, like Gilbert and Sullivan's Bunthorne, is thought absurd, if not outright silly. But the word itself has a much more profound meaning; it is derived from the Greek and its proper sense is the feeling-tones with which humans respond to that which speaks to them in their very depths, beyond the rational or logical or moral. Closely related to it is imagination, understood not as fanciful thinking (although we have seen that there are times when that is perfectly sound and right), but as a capacity to relate oneself fully to the truly attractive or good or lovely. We ought not to confine the use of the word aesthetic to art, although of course it includes our response to artistic creations.

The philosopher Alfred North Whitehead has much to teach us here. In his great book *Adventures of Ideas,* as well as in his Lowell lectures, *Science and the Modern World,* he insisted that the aesthetic is so much part of human experience that its neglect will seriously damage harmonious development. He would have been the last person in the world to reject scientific inquiry, since he himself started life as a mathematician and continued it as an expert in the philosophy of science. He was keenly aware of the moral dimension of human life and he valued highly the religious attitude toward the world. But in his view, science was often too narrow and abstract; morality was often too hidebound by convention; and religion could become mere dogma that stifles the human spirit. However, he felt that *genuine* religion had a certain similarity to the aesthetic attitude. And it was this aesthetic attitude that he esteemed for its supreme importance to us in our attempt to understand ourselves and our world.

Another distinguished thinker and writer of our time, F.C.S. Northrup of Yale University, has spoken in much the same way in his *The Meeting of East and West*. Dr. Northrup thinks, rightly I believe, that a long-continued defect in Western culture has been an overemphasis on the rational and ethical and an underemphasis on the aesthetic. He contrasts the European and American stress on rationality and morality with the oriental, or Eastern, stress on what he styles "the aesthetic component" in the world. He might have developed at rather greater length the typical Western tendency to harp continually on the ethical aspect of life. Our culture has been disproportionately intellectualistic and moralistic; it has given inadequate recognition to the lovely, the harmonious, and the delightful, all of which evoke the aesthetic response in humans. The result has been an overly calculating, chilly, unemotional view of things. Because each of us *is* an aesthetic creature, however, our deeper feeling-tones have never been entirely suppressed.

Both Whitehead and Northrup have urged that education in the West should recognize this fact and concern itself much more with the development in children and young people of the aesthetic response to life. Their comments remind one of Sir Herbert Read's argument that art is absolutely central to good education. And we must agree with what all these scholars have said. Fortunately, in their reaction against our decent and respectable bourgeois inheritance, many of today's younger generation have discovered this for themselves. Yet it is rather tragic that so many of us must attend courses in what is called "sensitivity training" before we can grasp something that is so integral to true human existence.

The aesthetic is closely related to love. For love is not primarily a matter of the intellect. Nor is it concerned so much with moral issues, if by this we mean the conscientious performance of duty according to ethical principles imposed upon us. Whitehead himself once said that "love is a little oblivious of morals"—and for this saying we should be grateful. Morality should not be, but often is, judgmental and censorious. Rationality can be abstract and cold. We need to approach life in a warmer and more emotional fashion. Love and the aesthetic response have their enormous role in fulfilling our existence.

In order to live in the world we must explore it so that we can know more about its functioning and make the necessary adaptations. We must also explore human personality, so that we can understand it and better grasp the meaning of human behavior. There is nothing wrong with such an enterprise. Similarly, we must often exploit the world to provide opportunity for growth—although here we have had so much exploitation that nature itself is rising up against us in what we nowadays call the ecological crisis. It may even be that we have to exploit other people, if by this we mean only our using their capacity to work and to make their contribution to the common good—but here, too, there is a danger of which we are increasingly conscious.

In the last analysis, however, neither exploration nor exploitation is the ideal way of responding to our situation as those who are becoming fully human in association with their fellows and in a world which we must accept as our home. I suggest that the right attitude is one that I may describe as *expectation*. By this I mean a delighted, deeply felt, reverent openness to others and to the world, and even to oneself. This is an open and eager entrance into relationships, with the urgent desire that some freshness will emerge from "deep down things," as Gerard Manley Hopkins put it. Because this is an active and positive attitude, it requires willingness on our part to do all in our power to help this freshness to reveal and express itself.

In this sense, love is expectant; if it is not, it can

resemble the use of others for one's own gratification rather than for mutuality, sharing, giving-and-receiving. The expectant man or woman, sensitive to others and responding to them emotionally as well as in other ways, is eager and accepting. He or she finds delight in others. He or she reverences them for what they have it in them to become; and he or she reverences also the things *they* reverence, even if those things do not happen to have personal appeal. He or she has an urgent desire for the best good of others. Thus we can see how closely related the aesthetic and the loving must be.

Play, amusement, and humor; relaxation, refreshment, and recreation; love and loving relationships: all these have their aesthetic quality since all involve our feelings. How odd it is that so many of us can only distrust our feelings! Of course we know that *some* feelings are not to be trusted—but that is also the case with some of our supposedly logical conclusions or rational ideas, not to mention our moral judgments. But feeling *as such* is part of what it means to be human; indeed it is a very central part, without which being human is sheer impossibility. The satisfaction that accompanies the realization of potentiality and the entrance into shared life with others as we move forward in becoming whole persons in love, is something *felt,* rather than something to be rationalized, moralized, or talked about.

5

Human Beings as Lovers

I HAVE DISCUSSED the way in which work can contribute to the realization of human potentiality and have spoken of the contribution made by play and amusement as a relief from the continuing pressure of work and as a means toward richer personal development. Now I turn to the capacity for love, so deeply imbedded in human existence that it is in fact the basic clue to what it means to be human here and now in this world.

Love is a matter of relationship. The relationship may be with one's husband or wife, with one's children, with one's friends, with neighbors; it may be with the person whom we call our lover. In these various kinds of relationships we get out of, and are delivered from, self-regarding interests and concerns. We are enabled to enter into the contact with others that is integral to our wholeness. Later I will discuss some of these types of love (family, friends, neighbors, and "other people"). Now, my attention is given to the love that has a specifically sexual element. I have insisted that *all* love has a sexual quality, simply because of the human constitution as a mind-body-emotion complex. But in certain modes of loving the sexual element is very central indeed.

In much writing about human love there has been a conspiracy of silence so far as this sexual element is concerned. Various reasons may be given for this silence. Sometimes it is because a writer takes a negative attitude toward it. He or she may think that sex is dirty, not to be mentioned in polite society. Even in our own supposedly enlightened day, there are some who are offended by the fact that they are sexual beings. They would prefer to keep this hidden; or, if it must be mentioned at all, their tone of voice indicates fear of the subject or contempt for the fact. They are scandalized when the human sexual organs are portrayed in works of art or when their function is mentioned in books. This is not because good taste suggests that some things should not be flaunted before the public. That would be understandable. But for these people it is because sexual matters are considered nasty in themselves.

Sometimes the silence about sex is based upon an overly spiritual view of human beings. For many years it was taken for granted that we are essentially souls who happen, for a short period, to inhabit physical bodies but for whom those bodies are merely temporary dwelling places that have no integral relation to the meaning of our humanity. The body's nature and function were thought to be unimportant in the portrayal of essential human nature, save insofar as they inhibit the soul's freedom by imposing physical limitations upon it. When the ancient Greeks thought in this way, they used a phrase about the body being "the prison-house of the soul." Still other people follow, probably unconsciously, the kind of philosophy associated with thinkers like Descartes, the great French philosopher who spoke of mind-stuff (*res cogitans*) as quite separate from matter-stuff (*res extensa*), and hence set up an intolerable dualism at the heart of human experience. Such a view has been described by the twentieth-century British philosopher Gilbert Ryle as the theory of "the ghost in the machine." Ryle has rightly criticized this dehumanizing idea.

In many different ways, then, people who should have known better have taken a low view of the human body and hence of sexuality. They talk in terms of ideals and values and assume that these have nothing to do with the sticks and stones, the dirt and dust, the physical and material aspect of the world. They forget that we never know beauty save as it is expressed in some person or thing, nor goodness save as it shows itself in good actions, nor truth save as it is stated in some form—nor even love, save as it has its observable manifestation in things said and done.

This *overly* spiritual attitude is mistakenly assumed to be very religious. This may be the case with some of the world's religions, but so far as Christian culture is concerned it is highly unreligious, since that culture is based, religiously speaking, on a faith that sees God in a human life and worships God through material things like the bread and wine of the communion service. Yet it is true that during a long period of Christian history there has been a certain fear of the body and of sex. It would be unfair to blame only the Puritan tradition for this, since history shows that this negative attitude goes back to the early days of the Christian religion.

Distrust of the body and sex originated in what scholars call "gnosticism," a philosophy prevalent in the Graeco-Roman world at the time Christianity made its appearance. Because this philosophy was so widely held by thoughtful people of the time, the first few centuries of Christian thought were influenced by it, although the church never accepted it. The Gnostics simply did not like the material world. It was less real than the spiritual one, they thought. Because it was less real it was less worthy, and anyone who wished to be truly spiritual should concentrate on spiritual matters and adopt a negative attitude toward the body. The result was a thoroughgoing rejection. The body must be denied in practice and, so far as possible, put firmly in its place. Marriage was a poor second best; virginity, understood as complete abstention from all sexual expression, was the better way. In its exaggerated forms, the discipline of the body included fasting to the point of near starvation, mistreatment of the body by flagellation, the wearing of hair shirts to kill desire, and a host of other devices to prevent the body from asserting itself. Only in this way, thought those Christians who were influenced by gnosticism, could any progress be made toward the truly Christian life.

Such an attitude toward the body is thoroughly unbiblical. It contradicts the main emphasis of the Jewish tradition that Christianity inherited and canonized when the Jewish scriptures (the Old Testament) were included with early Christian writings to compose the Bible as we know it. The Jews believed the body and the world and human sexual life to be good things because they were all created by a good God. Christians agreed and added the belief that, in Christ, God had "taken flesh" in a man. The early church fought hard against the Christian version of gnosticism, which was then known as Docetism: that is, fleshly things are merely an "appearance," and not truly real. But as so often happens, Christian thinking was itself affected by the very thing that it wished to reject. Unconsciously, the great leaders of the early church were influenced by the Hellenistic tendency toward gnosticism. The Judeo-Christian insight about the goodness of world, body, and sex was altered to fit in with the nonbiblical conception. In consequence, for hundreds of years it was assumed, and in some quarters it is still assumed today, that the devout Christian should disregard the bodily side of existence, above all the sexual aspect. Of course, it has never been possible to do this completely, so various kinds of concessions have been made, but they have always been regarded as a second best. Only recently—within, say, the last hundred years—has there been a return to the early and healthy Judeo-Christian attitude.

When alarmed observers of the current scene note how young people accept their bodies with delight and find joy in the sexual expression of their bodily desires, they should remember the repressive tradition that preceded the modern revolt. As we all know, one extreme leads to another. The utter denial of the body has brought about a reaction of utter freedom in the use of the body. This should have been expected. Some of us, including myself, think that the present openness and acceptance is much healthier than the former negation. Yet a middle position is possible, one in which the body and sexuality are gladly accepted and frankly enjoyed, along with a recognition of the need for controls so that the physical sexual life may help and not hinder growth toward responsible and satisfying realization of sexuality as a way to human self-fulfillment.

If we are ever to understand human nature, and above all its sexual drive, we must see men and women in their complexity: mind and body, soul and stuff, spirit and sense. Against those who would stress mind, soul, spirit, we must stress body, sense, stuff—and *vice versa*. Only so can we hope to recognize what human loving involves. Furthermore, when the moral dimension in being human is taken into account, it can never overlook this same complexity. If it does it will be inadequate, so inadequate that it is false. We shall then be talking about an imaginary creature called by the name "human," but who is not really human at all. As we have seen earlier, the complete denial of sexual selfhood, attempted by those who for one reason or another have found it unpleasant, produces a sinister distortion of our humanity, a twisting and warping, whose end product is the "spinster," male or female. The sourness that is manifested there is a frightful thing to behold; it is destructive of the person and damaging to those with whom that person comes in contact. It spreads and affects others so that presently we have the spectacle of nasty men and women who poison the corporate life of which they are part. In their attempt to kill their sexuality, they fail to achieve what they are seeking. Their sexuality is not destroyed or killed but thrust deep down into their unconscious lives where it festers and then finds entirely bad means for expression. It emerges as bitterness, suspicion, contempt, and hypocrisy. These make existence miserable for everyone, save perhaps for the person who is thus repressed. But even that person, precisely because he or she has succumbed to bitterness and the like, has lost the chance for healthy, sane, and free relationships with others. The snooper, the voyeur, the captious critic of behavior, the malicious gossip are the victims of their repression and the carriers of an infection that can poison any group. Alas, the repression is sometimes not their own in the first instance, but has been induced by bad teaching in early years or by continuing misrepresentation by others of the truth about our human nature.

We should gladly affirm our human bodies. Those bodies are ourselves, just as much as are our minds or spirits. In affirming them we are also affirming that sexual instincts, drives, and desires are integral to human life. Thus, a partial definition of human existence is that it is sexual. Human sexuality is not identical with that of other creatures, of course; it is not the same as that of the ape or the apple. Nonetheless, it is real; it is what we *are*, among the other things that we are. Once this is granted, we can begin to work out a pattern of human nature that will find place for this central sexual element.

Consider how we are made up or constructed. Physically each of us is a certain integrated patterning of energy —electrons, atoms, and molecules. Physiologically we are living organisms, functioning in bodily fashion like all other animals. We are possessed of the various systems which make that functioning possible: nervous, respiratory, digestive, reproductive. Biologically we are impelled to seek union in a sexual way with others of our kind. We are equipped with glands that serve this purpose and we have the sexual organs that make it possible for us to unite our bodies. So, psychologically, we wish to be with others and our drives are directed toward this end. Our emotions, with their physiological base, are psychologically directed toward such sharing. Thus the human organism in its wholeness is ordered for the expression of our selfhood.

But there is even more. Mentally and spiritually, we are so made that we must live with others; and it is our urgent desire, when we are developing normally, to seek to go out of ourselves in participation with others of our species. This fact crowns the pyramid of uniting tendencies or drives. Taken as a whole, the picture that we now have of our humanity is a more or less fully integrated one. And we can readily see how the sexual aspect pervades the whole picture; its physiological, biological, and psychological elements are the ground or basis for the conscious urge toward union.

Biologically, of course, the purpose of human sexual organs is to be united so that our species may be continued by the production of offspring. In this respect we are no different from other animals. But in us the sexual quality has been modified in such a way that it is not merely a matter of reproductive functioning. It is not only the means for the continuation of the species. Much more significantly, it has become the way in which sharing of life in tenderness and mutuality can be achieved. So far as we know, we are the one species for which this is a possibility, although there may be dim intimations of it in other species. The human sexual urge is not confined to periods when reproduction is possible. Neither is a man or woman driven only by the strength of a physical need that must be met in a sexual fashion. Our sexuality is more than a matter of release of tension. It includes that, naturally; but it is essentially an expression of the deep desire to achieve union with another, such as will further our own and our partner's fullest realization of the possibilities of being human. The sexual contact enables two persons to discover mutuality at the deepest level of giving-and-receiving, to share life together in the richest sense, when their bodies are united as an instrumental means for the uniting of their total selves.

Thus human sexuality is primarily the way for the expression of love. It is the condition which makes love a genuine possibility; it is the natural basis for it. This is true of every kind of loving in which humans may engage. Even in relationships that commonly are thought to have no sexual or even physical basis at all, there is some kind of sexuality, however slight, as a component. There can be no escape from this, even if we wished it. And why should we wish it, if sexuality is so deeply a part of total human personality in the making?

When I was a schoolboy I read with some surprise, in a book written by a wise and experienced schoolmaster, that in all friendship there is a sexual aspect. The writer was honest enough, and brave enough, to say frankly that when two boys or two girls in a single-sex school find themselves attracted to each other, a physical aspect is undeniably present. He urged that this be understood from the start, since it would help young people to order their relationships so that they would not fear whatever sexual overtones might appear to their conscious minds. Then they would not be unduly disturbed if, in some way, that element expressed itself. They would be delivered from the terror or horror which sometimes disturbs young people when this happens. Furthermore, schoolmasters, parents, and others concerned with them would be assisted by recognition of this fact, and would not be alarmed by intimate friendship or be afraid that "the worst" might happen. Once such an awareness is more general, he believed, children would be allowed to grow up naturally, without the damaging repression of their instincts; they could be counseled intelligently about finding appropriate kinds of relationships. Through free decisions, they could determine what is right for them in growing up, rather than experience the fear and alarm associated with the possibility of doing what is said or thought by others to be wrong.

The same point may be made about relations between young people of opposite sexes. Today, some sort of sexual experimentation is almost inevitable. We need not approve all attempts at such experimentation, but we can be realistic enough to see how young people are made and how they feel impelled to act. Realism makes it possible, as the negative attitude does not, to assist them in understanding the need for responsibility in their decisions and hence to decide upon the sort of activity that will bring them both to fuller and finer manhood and womanhood. Probably there is general agreement today that this approach is far healthier, as well as far more effective, than a negative and repressive attitude. We know that the latter is almost certain to provoke violent outbreaks of exactly the type that the parent or counselor or teacher is trying to avoid.

A similar approach is desirable in respect to autoerotic acts or masturbation. The practice is almost universal, as we now know. If and when it becomes an habitual *substitute* for relationships with other people, it can be psychologically and spiritually harmful. But when it is primarily a relief of sexual pressure or tension, it is harmless.

Happily, very few people today would tell boys and girls that the practice is likely to lead to blindness, stunted growth, and all manner of ill. We have every reason to be grateful for this change in approach. There is no occasion, of course, to urge masturbation upon children or young people; most of them, especially males, will occasionally engage in it anyway. But it is necessary for older people to realize that there is no cause for them to be greatly disturbed about it; rather, they should accept it for what it is. The great majority of young people give it up, at least as a regular practice, as they grow up. In any event, nobody can overdo masturbatory acts, since the physical organism sets its own limits. The only harm comes when such acts, whether by younger or older persons, are a sign of withdrawal from mutuality and giving-and-receiving with others. Then the practice can distort the proper development of human beings toward the fullness which is meant to be theirs; and that fullness, we need hardly repeat, involves genuine sharing of life with others.

Like everything else that is good, sexuality can be twisted and perverted. Such distortion is usually found in ways different from those conventionally condemned as wrong. The truth of the matter might be put in this way. Sexuality is wrongly expressed when it is without regard for the other person involved. It is wrongly expressed when the other is treated simply as a means of self-gratification and not as a person whose fulfillment is to be helped and shared. It is wrongly expressed when it is cruel: either sadistic, by a desire to hurt others, or masochistic, by a desire to be hurt oneself. In such cases love is not really present, save in the subtle sense indicated by the great teacher who said that nobody ever seeks what is wrong simply because it *is* wrong but always because at the time it *seems to him somehow good*, even though the good may be so misunderstood that it is disproportionate and can be damaging both to oneself and to the person from whom one seeks it. Such love can be called *sheer lust*—and again I stress the adjective sheer to make plain that lust, as such, is simply strong desire and is not bad, but good and natural and normal in human nature. What is needed in all human sexual matters is control, not negation or repression.

Most human beings desire to express themselves sexually with a member of the other sex: men with women, women with men. That is what courtship and marriage are all about, with the final establishment of a family, about which I will talk in the next chapter. But we cannot forget that there are some men and women—the experts say something like 5 to 10 percent of the total population —whose desire for love and its physical sexual expression is with persons of the same sex. These men and women are sexually attracted to other men and women, respectively; it is only with them that they can experience the deepest love and enjoy its sexual acts. They are called homosexuals, a word which comes from the Greek word *homo,* which means same, and the Latin word *sexus,* sexual desire.

For far too long, homosexuals have been reviled, condemned, attacked, punished, and at one time (if they were males) likely to be put to death if they acted on their urgent sexual desire. Yet, in every way, homosexuals are simply ordinary human beings, like their fellow men and women, save for this one difference in sexual orientation. Fortunately, attitudes have changed, and increasingly, in almost every part of the world, the homosexual is being accepted as a human being who has the same rights and the same responsibilities as his or her heterosexual brothers and sisters. The experts disagree as to the origin of homosexuality. But the fact is that homosexuals are what they are and most of them do not wish to be otherwise. This is not because they necessarily rejoice in their difference; but because they find in this particular kind of sexual expression a good and joyful way of being themselves. Attempts to change them against their will are almost always destructive of their personality. The effort to force them into marriage is almost certain to produce misery for both marriage partners. The homosexual needs from others recognition of his or her particular condition, not as something wrong or evil, not as something diseased and regrettable, but as something that for him or her is good. The homosexual needs help, as do all men and women, in realizing human potentialities, whatever they may be, and in doing this in association with others who share that sexual inclination. To put it in the simplest way, following the whole argument of this book, the homosexual should be helped to find in love the meaning of being human—and for a homosexual this will be discovered in a love that expresses itself in relationships with persons of the same sex.

I write at some length on this matter for three reasons. First, for the sake of the homosexual, because I am convinced that he or she needs much more understanding than is usually given. Second, because I am equally convinced that there is an element of homosexuality in all close friendships between persons of the same sex, as there is an element of heterosexuality in such friendships between persons of opposite sex. When we understand this, we can better see the significance of human friendship and be less fearful of its possible sexual component. We can be delivered from the fear that true and healthy friendship must of necessity be dispassionate, almost chilly, and certainly detached. Of course, in most friendships there is no overt sexual expression; yet the sexual element is there and we are the better for having recognized its presence. A little experience and a little observation should have taught us this. But it is astonishing to discover how often it is forgotten or overlooked. That is why we are frequently presented with a picture of friendship that has about it the coldness we find in the ideal of friendship painted by Aristotle when he idealized the man who is aloof and uninvolved, yet who condescends benevolently to be with and to assist others. This is hardly the type of human being whom we really admire or whom most of us would care to emulate.

The third reason I have given attention to homosexuality is that it helps us to see something about love that always needs to be remembered. We need not subscribe to the silly claim of some homosexuals that their sort of love is necessarily better and finer than love between heterosexuals. Yet in homosexual affection there is or can be something very beautiful. By the very nature of the sexual expression of homosexual love it is impossible to produce offspring. It can be creative in a wider sense, however. The sexual contacts may be most intimate, involving the sexual organs in almost every way, except the way that results in conception. And that brings us back to the recognition that for the human species love is *not* primarily for the purpose of reproduction, even if in heterosexual contacts that is the frequent result. The real purpose of sexual relationships is union and sharing, what I have called mutuality and giving-and-receiving at the deepest level of the two selves.

Yet it is obviously true that in most acts of heterosexual union a likely consequence could be the bringing into the world of another human life. This, too, is a very good thing. It is an illustration of the fact that goodness, which in this instance is the goodness of the sexual act, is diffusive of itself. It creates—here, it procreates—that which is not itself. The joy of parenthood, the delight in bringing up one's children, the establishment of a family cell of love, are of the greatest importance. Nonetheless, we must remember that what distinguishes humans from animals in the matter of sexual life is precisely that mutuality and sharing upon which I have laid such stress.

Procreation does not need to take place as a result of every sexual contact between a man and a woman. Nowadays, thanks to scientific discovery and technological invention, it is possible to prevent the conception of an undesired child. Here we are not concerned with which contraceptive methods are most desirable for controlling birth and planning a family. We simply assert that such methods exist and that they are used by a growing number of men and women who feel that their sexual relationships must not always result in the birth of a child, but can be enjoyed for their own sake as a genuine expression of their love and as a way of deepening that love. This is a good thing, especially because it makes possible responsible choice in the matter of procreation.

In all sexual union, what takes place is a deepening, enriching, and strengthening of tenderness, sharing, and the giving-and-receiving that love is all about. I have said in all sexual union; I should qualify this by excepting the *merely* self-gratifying, cruel, and unaffectionate instances of such union. Yet even there, I think, something may be learned—if painfully. For the frustration, the futility, and the furtive nature of such distortions of sex may lead some people to a more wholesome and sound understanding, and bring them to see that love is more than they had taken it to be.

I return at the end of this chapter to the point made all along: love is the clue to the meaning of being human. Through love, humans become more and more human. Through love, they are enabled to realize more adequately their potentialities and find the wholeness or integration that, however unconsciously, they seek and desire. Through love, human relationships in the community are made fuller and richer. Human sexuality, upon which this love is based, is more than a part of human existence that may be disregarded or forgotten. It *is* human existence seen from one point of view. Hence it is to be accepted as such, not grudgingly but joyfully. An ancient Hebrew scripture says, "It is not good for man to be alone." Sexual desire and sexual acts are bound up with this truth that the Hebrew scripture so succinctly states for us. One can only wonder that anybody has ever thought or wished it to be otherwise, especially when one thinks of the enormous satisfaction, the great happiness, and the enrichment of life which human sexuality has given to men and women as they become more human and hence more themselves.

6

The Family

FOR THE GREAT MAJORITY of men and women the estate of marriage provides the intimate relationship within which they find their happiness. Through living together and sharing all that they have and are, including their sexual desires, they find the opportunity to develop their potentialities, realize wholeness, and move toward fulfillment. They find there the mutuality that is more enriching for them than the fulfillment that either could have achieved alone. When children are born to them as the result of their sexual union they have the possibility of joy in raising a family and discovering in the offspring, who are the creation of their love, renewed occasion for happiness.

Some do not or cannot achieve this family life. It may be because of a decision not to marry, on the grounds that the work to which they believe themselves called can be better done if they are free from the responsibilities that family life entails and can devote themselves entirely to their job. It may be through no wish of their own but simply that they did not meet the person of the opposite sex with whom they felt it possible to enter into a lifelong relationship. For such people, however deeply they may regret their not being married, a way can be found in which fulfillment and satisfaction is provided through relationships of a different sort: deep friendship, service to others, and the like. And there are the homosexuals, about whom I spoke in the preceding chapter. They are not attracted to persons of the opposite sex; if there is to be a union of lives, it must be with someone of their own sex. Such a union is not only possible but desirable for them; and there are many men and women who have been able to establish it. Such a union is not marriage, but it can be a good and splendid thing. It is unfortunate that until quite recently society has frowned upon homosexual union, when instead it should have sanctioned and welcomed it as a way in which the homosexual can find happiness and fulfillment. Nonetheless, as we have just noted, a homosexual relationship, even if it endures for many years, is not a marriage in the historical sense of the word and should not be regarded as such. For all men and women, however, genuine and deep relationship with another or with others is necessary to true growth. For most people, as we have said, this relationship is made possible in marriage and the family. It is with these people that this chapter is concerned; they constitute the perhaps 90 percent who are heterosexually inclined.

We need not discuss the way in which a boy and girl, or a man and woman, meet and fall in love. In Western culture today there is little if any coercion of the sort that still lingers elsewhere and at one time was common among us too. Very few if any marriages are arranged by parents or guardians. Young people marry because they themselves wish to do so. They meet each other, like each other, come to love each other, and decide to engage themselves to each other. Often there is something very lovely and deeply moving about this. It is beautiful to see a boy and girl who are in love. The look in their eyes, their joy in each other's presence, and their sometimes naive planning for the future, speak to depths in us that in their own way indicate how much such mutuality can mean, even to an observer.

The two young people marry. They may have made a mistake in doing so, of course. To err is human. If a mistake has been made, it should be recognized for what it is. Whatever we may think about the increasing incidence of divorce in modern times, most sane and sensible people would agree that when a marriage really is a failure, after every effort has been made to make it a success (and of course every effort should be made), it is far better to acknowledge the fact and act on it. To keep two human beings tied together when they have come to dislike, distrust, even to hate one another, is inhuman as well as stupid. An enforced continuation of their marriage can only produce a little cell of ill temper, bad relations, and bitterness that will have its effect on human society as a whole. The very atmosphere is poisoned. The dissolution of the marriage can have its evil consequences, too; these cannot be denied or disregarded. Among these unhappy consequences is a tendency, all too prevalent, to take marriage too easily, to lose sight of its intended permanence, and hence to bring about a degree of social demoralization. For after all, human society is founded on the basis of enduring relationships, with marriage as the chief among them. Furthermore, if children have been born of the marriage, they can sometimes suffer terribly through the separation that deprives them of normal family life.

In this chapter, however, I am not speaking of the problems which divorce may bring with it. I am speaking of the typical family in which the likelihood of divorce has not arisen and probably will never arise. The husband and wife *do* like each other, they *do* have common interests, they *do* wish to give and receive from each other. They are an ordinary married couple, trying to make their marriage as good as it can be. Probably they have two or three children whom they love dearly and for whom they are glad to make sacrifices so that their offspring may grow to full maturity in a happy and healthy home.

An important aspect of the normal marriage is its provision of what might be styled a school for the development or growth of human personality. That is not its intention, of course; people marry because they love each other, not because they want to improve themselves or others. Thank God for that! Sharing is what they have in view. The extra dividend, so to say, is in the development of selfhood which marriage can make possible. It is a gift, a by-product, the accompaniment of an estate sought, entered into, and enjoyed for other reasons. A sure way to ruin a marriage would be for one or both of the partners to think of it as a kind of mutual improvement association. Like most good and valuable things, that aspect comes by indirection. But it happens all the same.

When two people live together they must learn to accommodate themselves each to the other. In spite of the many things they share in an obvious way, each of them remains himself or herself. They may grow together so that characteristics of one rub off on the other: most of us have observed how in a couple married for many years there is a certain similarity of attitude, approach, and interest. Yet each has his or her own human peculiarities and idiosyncrasies—and that is good, since the relationship is enriched by sharing a diversity of interests and talents. Marriage is not a loss of selfhood; it is a way in which selfhood is realized in deep companionship with another at every level. A married couple will not always agree. How frightful it would be if they did! For that would indicate a suppression of distinctive personalities in an identity that makes real union of two in one an impossibility. Sometimes the disagreement may lead to quarreling;

but even that is not necessarily a bad thing, provided the quarrel is superficial and not a negation of the abiding relationship that holds the couple together in a mutuality that is valued and desired by both.

The one absolute essential in marriage is caring enough. In a well-known song by the Beatles, "She's Leaving Home," we are shown a horrifying example of *not* caring enough. Probably the reader remembers the song. It tells of a girl who has left home. Her parents cannot understand this. They can see no reason whatsoever for her departure, for to their minds they have given her everything they should have given her. She has had a home, provision for material needs, and everything else that she ought to have received in an obvious way. They are unaware of the fact, implicit in their lament at her departure, that the one thing they have not given her is a personal understanding of herself as a young girl in this modern world. And they have not given her *themselves*, in the deep sense of caring enough. So she felt that she must go away if she was to be herself and find herself in her personal integrity. The one thing necessary was awareness of that personal integrity, shown by those with whom she was immediately and intimately related.

The Beatles' song has to do with a child in the family. But similar failure is possible between husband and wife. It is all to easy to ascribe the blame to one party or the other in such cases. But quite apart from this difficult question of blame the tragedy of the situation is apparent. It is the tragedy of being closed in on oneself, with a resultant unwillingness to get involved in another's life in those places where the other really *lives*. We see this sometimes in those unhappy marriages where husband and wife certainly know all *about* each other, but where they do not seem genuinely to *know* each other. They cannot grow in mutuality because they are unable to achieve that mutuality in the first place. Hence neither of them can grow as a person who is to realize his and her potentiality as human. In the close relationship that family life establishes—in all its rich possibility—it is all the more necessary to seek mutuality and to enter into another's life. Between husband and wife, between parents and children, and in the total family circle, this is so important that without it a family can be hellish in its capacity to destroy personality or at least prevent the members from becoming whole persons.

A few years ago Sir Edmund Leach, then the provost of King's College, Cambridge, gave the Reith Lectures on BBC. In the course of one of these lectures, he spoke about the dangers in our modern nuclear family pattern. He may not have made his point sufficiently plain to the thousands of listeners, many of whom quite completely misunderstood what he was getting at. He was violently attacked, in an unreasonable fashion, by those who had failed to *listen* to his words, although in a manner of speaking, they had heard them. They were annoyed because he criticized a family style that they assumed to be given from on high. Yet what he said was of great importance. Speaking as an anthropologist who had studied patterns of society in different cultures, Sir Edmund noted that the modern narrowed family circle has a demonic aspect. In an older day the group was larger, very likely with grandparents, uncles, aunts, and others living together. But today there is more likely to be a situation in which husband, wife, and perhaps one or two children constitute the group. They know a great deal about each other. But in their knowing about each other they lack somehow the capacity for awareness which participation in a larger group would have supplied by giving them a wider context and deeper background. In other words, they know about each other far too well, through a loss of the sense of distinction between persons even in their intimacy. Hence they have their little domestic secrets which can never see the public light; they stew in their own juice.

What we need today is some substitute, or some way of making provision, for the loss of the larger family circle. Whatever the reasons for this development in our own time, the modern family seems to be peculiarly exposed to this "nuclear" danger. All the more reason, then, to listen to those who discern the danger; all the more need to work out healthy family mores and habits; and all the more necessity for striving earnestly after a mutuality which will respect the distinctive personhood of each member. To be forewarned is to be forearmed: if we know about the peril here, we may be able to take steps to avoid succumbing to it. This is not easy. But some things will help.

For example, all the members of a family may be given a share in the making of decisions which affect them. Obviously, in any family some division of responsibility and work is necessary. Somebody earns the money by which the family lives, somebody is particularly concerned with what we call homemaking. Yet willingness to discuss together family problems is entirely possible. To do this is to give those who are closely concerned the feeling that they *matter*. It is not impossible that even the youngest member, once given the chance, may make some useful contribution to the decisions. But even if he or she does not, there can be awareness of the child's presence and his or her ideas can be valued—and it is this that matters above everything else.

A family, whether large or small, is a society in which all the members play their part. Each member is himself or herself, and nobody else. Yet each member is also one of the little group. Each will become more fully a self as he or she realizes more fully the reality of social belonging. Conversely, the group will be enriched and its common life deepened as each member is helped toward proper development. In this way the family is the human race or human society in miniature. No one can truly exist without association with others. Nor can society be allowed to become a completely impersonal affair, like an ant hill. That would gravely damage those who belong to society for no longer are they seen as persons but only as those who mechanically perform required duties. Human society is not an ant hill; neither is it a mere aggregate of a great many individuals who happen to be together at one place and time. In a general sense a healthy society is one which is so ordered that it is not totalitarian in the sense of denying personal integrity to each member, nor is it a mere collection of people who have no real participation with one another. The way to avoid both dangers is for society to ensure that each member is accepted for what he or she is and for what he or she may become. The social group is the means through which fulfillment is augmented by the help one's fellows can give as together they have a common loyalty and strive for common goals. This is where the family counts for so much.

As Sir Edmund Leach noted, the nature of family life is such that it permits much greater intimacy than can be found in other types of human association. This intimacy has its dangers but it also provides a splendid opportunity for growth. The *danger* is that husband, wife, and children will know so much about each other that their sense of personality is endangered. Then there is no longer a relationship of union but a submerging of each in the totality. The *opportunity* is precisely the possibility of growth in the relationship of union, a relationship which pervades every part of the life of each member but does not destroy it. Nothing need be held back, but each is also a self moving toward fuller selfhood. Of each member we can say *he* and *she*; we can also say *they* of their close association together.

A couple I know sometimes speak of their marriage as a union of two lives to form one life. That is what love can accomplish for human beings. Yet it is the *two* who form the *one*; without the two the one would not be union but simple identity. For without some distinction, union is impossible; there is then only the same thing twice—and that is not union at all. Nor would it be an expression of love, if love means relationship and not sheer identity in which the lovers no longer exist as selves. We might phrase this by noting that the family relationship makes *separation* impossible, while it requires (and, if sound and right, helps to establish) genuine *distinctions*. This is no verbal quibble; it gets to the very root of the matter. I am *I*, you are *you*, together we are *we*—and in the family we are we in as full and intimate a relationship as is possible for men and women and children. This is the ideal. But, like all ideals, it might not be vividly realized nor completely achieved. That is not so important as the recognition that the intention is present and that we bend our efforts to make it a concrete fact in our shared experience. Nonetheless, it is not impossible to bring it to pass. Doubtless most of us have known families where the beauty of the common life is manifest and we have delighted in seeing it.

I have spoken of the division of responsibility in the family. Today, however, this is not the case in many families. Both husband and wife are wage earners, both go to work. Fewer families have the old division in which the husband was the breadwinner while the wife remained at home to keep house. *He* went to office, shop, school, or factory; *she* did the housework and took care of the children. In thinking about the family today we must take account of the change; and the ordering of family life must be accommodated to the newer situation. The new pattern may or may not seem to some people to be as satisfactory or desirable as the older one. Who can say? Evidently it is here to stay and we have to accept it as a fact.

In a family where both husband and wife are at work for most of the day, a different type of shared relationship is bound to appear. In former times, when John came home from work Mary was there to welcome him. He was supposed to be tired after a long and hard day on the job. She may have been tired, too, but it was thought proper for her to conceal any fatigue she may have felt. Nowadays both partners arrive home at about the same time, both of them weary from work, both wanting the welcome and refreshment of spirit that comes from return home. This is not easy to manage. From observation I would say that the likelihood of "nerves" and tension is much greater and there is a higher incidence of misunderstanding and petty squabbling.

But there is also a new opportunity for husband and wife to grow in their understanding of each other, to make allowances for each other, and to work out a way of helping each other. If they do not work out a relationship that provides for a new sort of pattern, the marriage will probably break up. Greater demands are made on each of them; more patience is required. The danger of a tragic end is balanced by the chance of growing together in a new way, as each does all in his or her power to care for the partner's needs, relieve anxieties, and make the home a place of acceptance and comfort.

In this new kind of situation the presence of children makes the matter all the more difficult. For the children are no longer at home with their mother for most of the day. They must be at school or receive care in a different way. But in the late afternoon they have returned home, as have their parents. The family is together again as a family. The possibility of a disordered and unhappy relationship is inevitable, since family life (especially for the children) is now a matter of but a few hours of the day. In the past the mother was likely to be on hand most of the time and children could count on her presence and assistance. Their father joined them later and took his part. No longer can this be the case when both parents are at work. But once again, if danger is there, so also is opportunity. Sharing of family life can be deeper because it is not taken so much for granted. If parents will make an effort, there may be gain and not loss.

One method that married friends of mine who both have jobs have found useful is to make the family's evening meal an occasion of some importance. It is not formalized at all, but it is a real gathering of those who are bound together in intimate love and concern. In addition to such a family meal, however, there can be sharing in some family hobby, making a trip together on weekends, going to the theater or movies as a family. Whatever it may be, it is a *family* enterprise. The old habit of reading aloud, now virtually forgotten, might be revived. Even watching a television show can be made a family affair, if the program chosen is the sort that appeals to all family members. In these and other ways real family identity can be established and strengthened.

An advertisement in the New York subways some years ago read: "The family that prays together, stays together." Here is still another way in which, through a common loyalty to a given faith, the unity of the family can be brought about. We might also change one word in that saying and make it read, "The family that *plays* together, stays together." I have argued that play is a proper part of human existence; it is one of the ways in which being human can become more meaningful, richer, and whole. Naturally this significance of play is not consciously analyzed when one is actually engaged in it. Hence when a family plays together, as it very well can learn to do, this will not be undertaken as a matter of intentional improvement; it will simply be for the fun of playing together. Nobody likes to be "improved" by others; indeed, when we try very hard to do this, the opposite may result. Any "improving" bit of play is likely to become boring; and far from bettering the characters of those who are its victims, it will worsen them. Real play with genuine enjoyment is different; it can be part of family life at its best.

As the children grow older they naturally want to be more "on their own." They wish to see their friends, go out on dates, and in other ways establish themselves as persons who are not totally dependent for their selfhood on their parents or others in the family circle. A good deal of tact is required from older people at this stage. Nothing can so effectively drive a young person from home as the feeling that the parents wish to *keep* him or her at home. The freedom that is indicated when a boy or a girl is given the key to the house is a mark of growing up; it is also a sign of the parents' trust. Trust is part of the love that is the meaning of being human. Not to be trusted is to feel oneself unloved, uncared for, regarded with suspicion. Young people cannot grow into the fullness of adult life if they feel that they are not trusted, and are always viewed with some slight suspicion. To them that means that they are neither loved nor respected for themselves. To show such trust, however, can be demanding on parents, especially when they know very well that their child may get into trouble of some sort. Yet freedom to get into trouble is also part of what it means to be human, more particularly what it means to be growing to maturity as a human being. Parents must take the risk: this is the way their deep love can show itself.

Nor can we forget that the occasion to take risks is present in the relationship of husband and wife. Failure of trust here can lead to "scenes" or to a feeling on the part of the suspected and distrusted person that happiness in self-expression must be sought elsewhere. Of course there is risk. But lack of trust is worse. It is one reason that some men and women seek the intimate companionship of another person outside the home, while others make a quick departure for a club or fraternal organization, a card party or social occasion, or wherever else they think there is a place for them to be accepted confidently, without question and without suspicion.

In any home where it can be provided, opportunity must be given for such privacy as each member desires. If possible, the children should have their own rooms to which they can retreat when they wish. Husband and wife, too, should have the opportunity to be alone when they want. Here is another manifestation of the principle of distinction without separation. It enables personal self-realization in social relationships without constant physical propinquity. We cannot emphasize too strongly that genuine sociality is not a matter of constant physical association. It is much deeper than that. A book published some years ago has the title *The Lonely Crowd.* This title is highly suggestive, for it is often the case that we feel most lonely in a crowd but not at all lonely when we are not physically with those whom we love because we realize that we are never truly separated from them. What is more, an occasional withdrawal, in a physical sense, can make the return to physical proximity all the more pleasant. We need to collect, and recollect, ourselves from time to time, so that we may make a fresh contribution to the social group. But throughout, there is a profound awareness of "togetherness" of heart and mind and spirit because this is *really* present, even during those moments when we enjoy being by ourselves.

One of the great joys of family life is to grow old together. Another is to see children grow up and make their way in the world. And a third is to welcome *their* children. A friend once said that the delightful thing about grandchildren is that one could enjoy them without feeling responsibility for them! Later on I will say something more about growing old gracefully; but for now, most of us would agree that the best way to do that is in the companionship, deepening through the years, of a person dearly loved, with whom we can share many memories. Somehow it seems that an old couple grows into each other more and more, so that in the end they may even come to resemble each other. This will make the death of one all the more difficult for the other; but there is surely compensation in increasing intimacy and in the sense that the years spent together have been good, satisfying, and rewarding.

Some of us who are not married miss a great deal of happiness. Yet there is a possibility of finding a family in another sense. Here I speak from experience. For I myself have never married, although at one time it seemed likely. Hence I do not have a family of a wife and children. But I have been fortunate in my profession. As a teacher I have been able to live in colleges where there was a common life in which I could share. I discovered that in one sense I *could* have a family of sorts—that family was made up of my colleagues and *their* families, of other senior members also unmarried, of junior members or students, and of those employed in the business of providing for the needs of three hundred or more people living together in the college.

The healthy life of a unit like that requires mutuality and concern for the welfare of the group and for each of the members, senior or junior; acceptance of each person as she or he is; provision of the necessary amount of privacy; activities to be enjoyed together; and the granting of freedom to make mistakes. No healthy college, for example, can be maintained by the expedient of ordering people around, nor can it be a happy place unless its members are allowed to be themselves, to develop each for himself and herself, and to find a proper way of realizing potentialities. At the same time, such a community must have a spirit of its own that is inclusive of everyone—an esprit de corps, as we might style it. All this means that love must be present, that diffused kind of love which is possible where one helps all and all are ready to help one.

I have known two of these larger groups, each for a number of years. In one of them, unfortunately, there was a slightly repressive atmosphere because those in authority were not always trustful of the juniors. The life of the community was unhappy from time to time, and on some occasions the strong pressures from above threatened to provoke a reaction of sheer anarchy among those below. By contrast, in the other college there was ready acceptance of the members, with no rules beyond the few necessary for the continuation of the work for which the college existed. There was a friendly spirit between seniors and juniors, the former trusting the latter and the latter feeling that the former were genuinely concerned for them. All were free to come and go as they wished, save for the necessary fulfillment of college obligations. One thing that always struck me was the acceptance even of mistakes. These were regretted, of course, but they were interpreted as due to lack of experience on the part of juniors or as unintentional errors of judgment on the part of the seniors. The atmosphere was relaxed and easy. In the navy, such a group is said to be a happy ship; we were really a happy family.

Whether we belong to a typical family of husband, wife, and children, or to the union of persons of the same sex, or to the less common one of a group, our family must promote, in every possible way, the movement toward human fulfillment in a relationship in which love is central and, therefore, where giving-and-receiving is found. Such a family can be a powerful symbol of the meaning of being human. It can help each member to see and act upon the love that is so necessary for human existence. Only as we live together in this way can we become fully human.

7

Having Friends and Being Friends

INGMAR BERGMAN, the distinguished Swedish film-maker, was once quoted in *Varsity* (a Cambridge University undergraduate publication) as having said this: "What matters most of all in life is being able to make contact with another human being. If you can take that first step toward communication, toward understanding, toward love, then you are saved."

I believe that Bergman here put his finger on something each of us deep down inside knows to be true. Relationship with another is indeed "what matters most of all in life." By phrasing it as he did, Bergman indicated his conviction that the grain of the universe runs with such relationship. He also is right in saying that taking "that first step," the first step toward love, is our way toward being "saved"—that is, toward grasping the meaning of being human and the manner in which we are redeemed from frustration, futility, triviality, and the like, whose effects on human existence are so deplorable. To be able to grasp this (even if we cannot put it into words) and to find ourselves somehow enabled to act on this basis, is the condition for our true becoming, our realization of potentialities latent in us, our coming to wholeness of life. For all this is possible *only* with others with whom we are "able to make contact." To take "that first step" is to open the door to continuing enrichment of life both for ourselves and for the human community.

Talk about being saved may be reminiscent of evangelical Protestant piety and its concern for moral "perfection." But the condition of salvation, in the sense in which Bergman surely intended it, is the condition of being on the way to true wholeness. In thoughtful religious circles, this is recognized when due account is taken of the derivation of the word salvation. *Salus* in Latin means health or wholeness; so does the equivalent Greek word *soteria*. In English, too, we have this same relationship, since "hale," "healthy," and "holy" all go back to a single Anglo-Saxon root. So we may conclude that salvation can mean something other than either moral perfection, on the one hand, or a proper labeling for heaven, on the other. It can perfectly well indicate two highly important things; first, a reverence before the mystery and wonder of the universe of which we are part, and before whatever power or energy is working through it; and second, a whole and healthy attitude toward our own existence and growth. In both respects, I repeat, *love* is the clue. For the deepest insight of all the great religious thinkers has led them to discern, sometimes dimly and sometimes vividly, that love *is* at the heart of things, while all of us, whether religious or not, can be brought to see that love is the truth of human meaning, that it is in fact the meaning of being human. So Bergman's use of the word saved is significant and helpful.

The poet John Keats once spoke about holiness (which, as we have seen, is related to wholeness or health and hence to salvation). He said that in understanding ourselves and others we need to remember "the holiness of the heart's affection." Loyalty and devotion to friends were for Keats at the very center of human living. His beautiful phrase is suggestive for our thinking about our friendships. The poet said that human beings really live in that "holy temple," as he styled it, whatever or wherever their physical home may be. The heart's affection is indeed a holy place and we shall do well to approach it reverently. The love of friendship, like other varieties of love, is not something cheap and superficial; it is a matter of human living in its depths.

The family is one place where true affection may be developed. But it is not the only place wherein we learn to live in love and hence to find the meaning of our being human. Friendship is another such place, and one of the most precious. An old adage says, "God gave us our family but we can choose our friends." The saying is not quite right, but it makes a point. For it is plain enough that in making friends we have the opportunity to exercise freedom of choice. Yet there is a strange fact about friendship that needs to be remembered. We do indeed choose our friends, but we receive their friendship as a gift. Nobody can *earn* a friendship, having decided that so-and-so is someone with whom he or she would like to establish this relationship. If one tries to earn it, one is likely to be dreadfully disappointed. One may assist the other, give gifts to that other, and in various ways try to win affection. Just possibly affection may result; but it is equally likely that one will receive gratitude but fail to receive genuine affection. In friendship, there is a combination of choice and gift which is mysterious and wonderful.

In all friendship, as in every other human relationship, there is a sexual element. It could not be otherwise, since we are possessed of an all-pervasive sexual drive that arises from our physiology and psychology and that finds its most complete expression in the specifically sexual act. Naturally, in friendship this act does not occur; but sexuality is present nonetheless. Its mode of expression must be appropriate to the particular circumstances of the relationship—in marriage, one way; in homosexual union, another; in friendship, still another. Failure to realize this truth can produce a fear of overly intimate association with others. We need to be realistic about this, to recognize ourselves for what we are, and to take account of our human constitution. I realize that some readers may feel that I have been altogether too insistent on human sexuality and its pervasive quality. I would answer them by saying that for far too long it has been forgotten or disregarded or condemned; and that nowadays we greatly need a sane and healthy stress on it, in order to arrive at a better understanding of ourselves and of our life with other people.

Few things have done more harm to the Anglo-Saxon character than the negative or repressive attitude to sexuality which the conventional boarding school has produced. Fearing overt homosexual activity, school authorities for more than a century have tried to bring up young people, especially boys, as if they were spiritual creatures dwelling in rugged physical bodies but without strong sexual drives. Or, when the drives have been recognized, they have been regarded as evil things, to be suppressed at all costs. The result has been exactly what might have been expected. Either the sexuality breaks out in some way and the guilty youth is expelled from school, sometimes with great scandal and usually with damage to his personality; or young people grow up, as E.M. Forster once said, with "an undeveloped heart":

The inhibited [Englishmen] go forth into a world that is not entirely composed of public-school men or even of Anglo-Saxons, but of men who are as various as the sands of the sea; into a world of whose richness and subtlety they have no conception. They go forth with well-developed bodies, fairly developed minds, and undeveloped hearts. And it is this undeveloped heart that is largely responsible for the difficulties of Englishmen abroad. An undeveloped heart —not a cold one.—*Abinger Harvest*, p. 5.

Notice the distinction between a *cold* heart and an *undeveloped* one: the heart of the average Anglo-Saxon may be very warm indeed, but often it has not developed so that he or she can enter into easy, open, and intimate relationships with others.

What Forster says about Englishmen abroad can be equally true of Englishmen at home. It can be true of Americans, Canadians, Australians, New Zealanders, and others of Anglo-Saxon background and education. When older people observe the freedom claimed by youth today, with their assertion of the right to love and their refusal to be regimented in a way that impedes open relationships with others, they are often horrified and think that all standards are being denied. What has happened, however, is very different. The young people are reacting against the conventional pattern of Anglo-Saxon education and training that their elders accepted and took for granted. The human spirit is asserting itself once again, after more than a century of repression. To them the conventional pattern of respectable society seems often a sham and a lie; they want nothing to do with it. Perhaps they exaggerate; certainly their way of reacting is sometimes violent and extreme. Yet there is truth in Robert Louis Stevenson's remark that "respectability is the deadliest gag and wet blanket ever devised for the free spirit of man." And when such respectability, which includes the "undeveloped heart," is thrust upon youth, demanded of them (as they think) if they are to be accepted by the community, rebellion is not surprising. I personally think that this revolt is a sign of their better understanding of human nature, both in themselves and in their contacts with others.

Thus I urge that no one be afraid to acknowledge the profoundly emotional tone in an intimate and true friendship. No one needs to feel ashamed of being attracted to another human being or of the way in which physical as well as psychological aspects are present in such attraction. Shared interests and tastes, similarity of outlook, circumstances that have brought us together, and much else enters into and establishes friendship. So does the sexual quality of human life.

Of course this does not mean that in friendship the partners usually engage in explicitly sexual activity, although this *can* happen. It *does* mean that the hand clasp, the touch, the embrace, can have their place on the proper occasions. A human being is an embodied creature, not a "spirit." The body is included in all that one is and does. How he or she expresses this will depend upon upbringing, good breeding, the attitude of the other, and the situation in which the two of them find themselves. Yet *some* sort of expression is good and healthy, if for no other reason than that the whole of us is open for, given to, and receptive of the other person. We have no reason to be frightened about it. After all, Latin peoples act in this way; and it is possible that Anglo-Saxons will do so naturally, too, once inherited inhibitions are overcome.

A first condition of friendship is a desire to give. But equally important is the willingness to receive. All loving relationship is two-way—a matter of mutuality in giving-and-receiving, to repeat once more the words I have so often used. An old teacher of mine once expressed this in a homely image: "Nobody likes a person who sets up the drinks and then says, 'No, *I* won't have any.'" It is more blessed to give than to receive, we have been told. Doubtless that is true. It is also true that it is often more difficult to receive, gracefully as well as gratefully. And it is supremely true that it is best to *share* with another as each gives and each receives. Certainly no true friendship can be developed on a *de haut en bas* attitude, in which I give to you but will not allow you to give to me.

Of course a friend is ready to give. A friend may give material things where the other is in need of them. A friend will give personal support where the other needs assurance. A friend will give the criticism which the other may also need, but this will be done with understanding. Above all, a friend will give himself or herself. And this is the heart of the matter. All of us want desperately to know that somebody cares for us; this is much more valuable than any amount of material assistance, important as that may be. But besides giving, the friend also shows a delight in receiving, for no true friend is too proud to admit dependence on the other. A true friend, then, will be glad to receive whatever the other can give, but, above all, will be overjoyed when from a friend there is the gift of self. As in all love, giving-and-receiving or sharing together is what matters most.

Many years ago I knew a young man and his family. The boy, in his late teens, was in all respects well-adjusted and self-sufficient. One would have thought that there was little if anything that he needed. During World War II he served in the navy and was on a ship in the South Pacific. During this period I had decided that I would write to him frequently since, like most young men in the armed services in distant places, he would doubtless be glad to receive letters. Then one day I had a letter from *him*. With it he sent me an autographed photograph taken at some naval base. I shall never forget what he wrote. He said that my letters, coming to him so regularly, had given him confidence and courage to go on with his perilous job, because he knew that somebody back home, apart from his parents, genuinely cared for him and continually remembered him. This, he said, had made all the difference. I was quite unworthy of his kindness in writing me in this fashion, for I had done very little for him. But I *had* remembered him, as he said; and I had not failed to keep in constant touch with him. In a very small way I had given him myself. (I apologize for telling this story; my only motive for doing so is that it provides an illustration from my own experience of what Samuel Johnson once called "keeping one's friendships in repair.")

There is no doubt that friendship must be cultivated. The giving-and-receiving must find some expression that will make it come alive. No friendship can simply be taken for granted. We should seek opportunities to live in and with the other. The little gifts on birthdays, the remembrance of special occasions important to the other, and (when the friends are separated) the writing of letters have all of them what we may call a sacramental significance. By this I mean that they are the outward and visible signs of the relationship. Through such things, as also through the appropriate hand clasp or embrace, an external action conveys the affection felt for the other. Letters or postcards are of special value when friends are at a distance from one other. A friend who cannot be bothered to write or in some other fashion keep the lines of communication open demonstrates that he or she has not grasped the simple fact that human beings are embodied creatures. Doubtless there are instances in which two friends after years of absence from one another and with no communication during that time can take up again where they left off. But I am fairly certain that this does not happen frequently.

To be a friend demands that we take trouble; and part of that trouble is constancy of communication. In keeping up with a friend and with that friend's ways of thinking and acting, we are in touch even when there are hundreds or thousands of miles between us. The relationship is deepened, the friendship cemented, and the next meeting is all the better and more fulfilling for both. And what joy such a renewed meeting can give after separation! To be with a person for whom one cares, to share in joys and sorrows, and to identify oneself with him or her in what makes the other what he or she is, is to realize that our love is real and carries on not only in spite of but also because of peculiarities, quirks, even defects. For it is the *person* whom we love. For a moment we may be annoyed or irritated by something a friend has said or done—but that is all right, since no one can expect complete agreement on everything. The very differences of opinion can deepen the basic relationship.

Like other kinds of love, friendship personalizes. The friend is no longer merely an individual, one of the human race with whom we happen to share a few interests and whom we meet from time to time. That would be acquaintanceship, not friendship. It is good to have acquaintances; it is essential to have one or more friends. And the personalizing effect of friendship can be remarkable. Because my friend is recognized and accepted as *this* person, just as he or she is and for what he or she is, my friend is enabled to become *more* of a person—that is, he or she is helped to realize more fully his or her potentialities and to achieve wholeness of life.

One of the changes that modern urban life has produced is a certain remoteness from others. Hundreds or thousands of people live close together but they do not know one another. There may be acquaintanceship, but friendship is more difficult to secure. In the next chapter something will be said about getting on with those acquaintances and with others whom we meet. Here we need only remark that no one can have a very large number of truly intimate friends. If one tries to have too many, one will spread oneself so thin that not much of one can be shared with another.

There is sense in the distinction made between "I-thou" (see page 106) and "I-you" relationships. In his book *The Secular City,* Harvey Cox used this distinction to point out the new situation in urban culture. He is right to do so, but it seems to me that he has failed to see that while we cannot have many genuinely "I-thou" relationships we must be on our guard lest the many "I-you" ones degenerate into an "I-*they*" kind. No one should be regarded merely as an object. Naturally in making large-scale calculations of an economic, sociological, or political sort, something like that seems to be necessary. But when we are in contact with other people it can be deadly and damaging.

Some years ago I was dining with a friend and his family. I met him at his office and went with him to his home, which was in an enormous apartment house in New York City. In the lobby of the great building there were dozens of elevators. We entered the one which served three floors high in the building, each with some eight or ten apartments. There were three other people with us, one of whom got off on our floor. I remarked afterward to my friend that I supposed he knew very well all the other residents on the floor and probably also those on the other floors served by that elevator. I shall not forget his answer: "Oh, no. I really don't know them very well. We're acquaintances, of course, and we pass the time of day. But if I tried to know them too well, to be friends with them all, I should not have any deep friendships at all. There *is* one chap I do know fairly well; but my friends live elsewhere." Since I knew him well enough I was able to make some comments on this lack of what I called neighborliness. To which he answered, "Don't misunderstand me. Of course we're neighbors and often we can do something for one another. But when I tried to take too many people into my circle of close friends, I found that I was beginning not to have any close friends at all."

His were wise words and I learned something from them. My only comment would be that (as I shall argue in the next chapter) we can and must seek to increase the personal element even in our acquaintanceships. In other words we can deeply love only a few and these are our friends. But this need not mean that we should reduce others to the horrible level of objects at hand.

How does one make friends? We touch here on a great mystery about human life, as mysterious in its way as falling in love on the road to marriage. I have said that physical attraction often enters into the picture. There is also a sharing of interests in work or play. There may be proximity: we may live near each other and hence see a great deal of each other. There may be many other causes and occasions. But we "fall into friendship" as we fall in love. That is to be expected since friendship is love in one of its modes. It just "happens," as love does. But of course we have to put ourselves in the way of making friends. Or, to phrase it more accurately, we have to let ourselves be put into that way, since this is no matter of our setting out determined to acquire friendships. Rather, it is a matter of being open to others so that such friendship may happen to us both.

To say that is to say that we need to make ourselves available. The man or woman who is closed in upon himself can never make friends, nor indeed have any intimate relationship of any kind. Psychologists speak of introversion, by which they indicate the condition of those who live so much inside themselves that they are unable to enter into real contact with what is outside. This can become pathological, with devilish consequences for the persons involved. Here we need to be careful lest we assume that the opposite of the introvert is the person who is entirely extroverted, so that he or she has little if any genuine inner life. We are selves and those selves are to be developed. That happens best when we link our selves with other selves in the human community. People who are totally self-centered deny common humanity with others. Such people are the living negation of the sharing which is to be ours; they can never make friends. They live too much in themselves, for themselves, to themselves, and by themselves. Such people are tragic figures who need help.

Perhaps some of us can supply the help needed. To be brought out of this tragic isolation, the hard shell of self-immersed existence has to be broken from the outside. Here only love can do the job. When I meet someone like that, I am given the chance to be available as and when I can, even if the experience is not very pleasant for me. I can show my concern in an unobtrusive way, although there may be no immediate response. I may do what I can to help in one way or another. Initial resentment must be expected. But the resentment is a manifestation of inner insecurity, a defense mechanism to protect from what is most feared: that someone will discover the inner vulnerability. Given time and persistence, as well as common sense, something can be done to help.

I have said that a person like this fears letting anyone else see this vulnerability. Still another point in true friendship is that a friend *is* vulnerable and can be hurt. Perhaps no one can hurt so much as the one most loved. This is not intentional hurt; but because the relationship is so close and so real, the words of an old popular song are true, that one always hurts the one one loves. What is more, *all* love has in it an element of anguish. We have spoken of this before; its reality is inescapable. Yet through the pain in love we become more human. We grow more sensitive and we learn to enter more deeply into the experience of others. The path to our wholeness is not smooth and easy; it has pain and disappointment. Yet there is no other way.

We return for a moment to availability. If it is necessary to be available in order to make friends, it is equally necessary in order to keep them. A friend is someone on whom you can always count, who will not let you down, who will be there when you need him or her. As A.E. Housman's poem says, "Whistle, and I'll be there." But availability is not only for the times of trouble, when the going is difficult and things seem dark and foreboding. It is *always* in the picture. This availability is much more than physical nearness; it is personal presence in even richer ways. Gabriel Marcel, the French existentialist, has written of what he calls "the sense of presence" that he believes to be much more spiritual than physical. Perhaps this is not the right way to put it; but the point is well-taken. It suggests an awareness of the other's surrounding care and concern, whether he or she be near or far.

This surely corresponds with our common experience. Think of the person with whom you are most closely related in love or friendship. That person may be hundreds or thousands of miles distant from you, or even on the other side of the world. Yet somehow she is there beside you, just where you are, for you know that she thinks of you and that she shares your life despite great distances between you. Such a sense of presence is indeed mysterious; it cannot be explained, or explained away, in scientific terms. If an attempt is made to do so, the friend or lover will laugh at the absurdity of the suggestion. For she or he *knows*, and has no doubt of its reality.

"A man is known by the enemies he keeps," it is said. Yes, perhaps. But he is known best by the friends he makes and keeps. We can learn a great deal about somebody if we know with whom he or she is friends. Superficial appearances may be harsh and hard, yet if anyone has some capacity for true friendship, that person is not *all* bad. Some years ago I was asked to write a biography of King Henry VIII. That Tudor monarch was not a very pleasant character and much about his life and activity was horrible. Yet as I plowed through the material on his life, I was immensely struck by two facts. One was that he had won the devotion of Thomas More: a man who could be friends with More must have had *some* good qualities, even if Henry later let his friend be executed. The other was that on his deathbed he wanted with him Thomas Cranmer, that good and gentle soul who made his mistakes but of whose fineness of character there can be little doubt. He died with Cranmer beside him, the chronicle says, after having wrung his hand as hard as he could.

The ancient Greeks had a variety of words to describe love. They spoke of *eros*, the love of strong desire; of *phileia*, the love of friendship; and of *storge*, familiar or family love. They were not afraid to see something of *eros* in the other two, although they drew distinctions among the three. They knew that "brotherly affection," or friendship, has its touch of *eros*. I have said that in all love, including friendly love, there is some element of sexuality. We have no reason to be ashamed of it; we need only see that it is rightly and appropriately expressed. What we need, then, is to develop our hearts, as E.M. Forster would put it. We need to see with John Keats that the "heart's affection" is holy. Above all we need to understand that it is through love, of any kind provided that it *is* love, that we most surely become human. Wholeness is our goal; and wholeness is living in love and becoming daily more and more the lover we have it in us to be. The love of friendship is an integral part of the total picture.

8

Getting On with People

O N THE TITLE PAGE of E.M. Forster's novel *Howard's End* appears the phrase: "only connect . . . ." This is, in fact, the theme of the novel. Forster is concerned to show that connection must be established between the seemingly opposing tendencies and attitudes found in human experience: between people of different classes, between romanticism and practicality, between youth and age, between feeling and reason. These opposites often keep people apart, destroy happiness, and ruin human society. To connect means to see things in their real relationship of contrast, not contradiction, and to accept them for what they may contribute to the enrichment of the common life. And this connection is not to be found in some prudently chosen middle path which carefully avoids all extremes, but in an awareness of the many-sided variety of human experience and the world, with a readiness and willingness to live in just such a situation.

What Forster is seeking to show in his powerful, moving, yet restrained story gives us the clue to getting on with people. If we ever hope to do this, we must be open to others, whoever and whatever they are, and be prepared to see in them potentialities that are to be recognized and esteemed. This means an attitude of love, not in the intensive sense of the word but in the more diffused sense of genuine good will and interest, which, in its degree and measure, will do exactly what we have said love always does: personalize those with whom we have to do. I remember a former student who once said of a teacher: "He treats us as *people*, not just as students." By this he meant that this particular teacher looked upon and treated all of his students as more than objects arranged in rows in a classroom; he saw them and acted toward them as persons to be respected and esteemed.

If we hope to get on with our neighbors and with the many others with whom we come into contact, we must learn to treat them in this way. Naturally it is impossible to have with them the intimate relationship we can enjoy with members of our family, our lovers, or our close friends. But it *is* possible to see each of them as possessed of potentialities that can be realized, recognizing in them a drive toward fullness or wholeness, and meeting them with the desire to care for or be concerned about them. This attitude can be adopted in respect to every man, woman, or child with whom we come into contact. It is just this attitude which makes human living-together in society decent and healthy. Without it, such living-together would be nothing but veiled conflict, sometimes even open but undeclared warfare.

When we consider the great problems that the world faces, all this may seem a very little thing. After all, there are the big issues of economics, politics, international relations, and the like, not to mention the hard questions that arise in our business or school or in our town or city. Yet many of us have known people who are so concerned with these supposedly big matters that they are extremely difficult to live with—even their families find them so. It is in such seemingly little ways that the real person is most fully revealed.

I have already mentioned the distinction between the "I-thou" and "I-you" types of relationship. The former, as I suggested, is possible only with a few people; it would be absurd to try to adopt it with everyone we meet. But if we hope to get on with these others we *must* see them in the "I-you" way. This is much less intensive, much less directly personal, much less intimate. But it indicates that we do not think of others, nor act toward them, as if they were *things* with whom we relate ourselves in the "I-they" style. They are not in the second-person singular; but neither are they in the third-person singular or plural. They are, so to say, in the second person plural, which means that they are seen as *people*. To treat them in that "I-you" way is to be moving in the direction of regarding them as in the "I-thou" category. Our relationship with them is such that the "I-thou" is not entirely ruled out in advance of any conceivable development in the relationship. If human life is always a *becoming*, it is a movement in one direction or another. What matters is the direction in which it is moving. In our contacts with others this is equally true. Are these contacts such that they might one day be more intimate and directly personal? Or, are they such that the direction is toward thing-hood?

The phrases "I-thou," "I-you," and "I-they" come from the great twentieth-century Jewish thinker Martin Buber. In his book called *I-Thou*, Buber makes the point that the distinctive quality of human relationships is that an "I-thou" attitude is conceivable and possible with any and every person, even if it may not be actualized in this or that particular instance.

Let us say, for example, that John Smith is my neighbor. He lives next door to me. I see him almost every day. I talk with him now and again about commonplaces, about what is happening on our street or in our part of town.

Sometimes I can be of help to him and he to me; perhaps we can borrow from each other when need arises. Both of us belong to the local residents' association. We have common problems to consider in respect to our neighborhood, and we may discuss these matters. In these and in many other ways we have a continuing contact. Of course we are not intimate as I am with my wife and family, if I have them, or with my close friend Stephen who lives some distance away. My relationship with John Smith, and his to me, must be more formal. But we cannot leave it there, since life is always on the move. Neither of us wants the direction of our relationship to be toward the *kind* of formality in which each will be for the other only one object among many other objects in the vicinity. Its direction should be *toward* more closely shared concern; that is, *toward* "I-thou," although very probably it will never reach that point. Thus the question which both of us must face is whether we are willing to know each other better, understand each other more thoroughly, share each other's interests more fully, and help each other more often and in better spirit. If we are, then we are good neighbors; if we are not, we are lapsing into the inhumanity which eventually may put us behind walls of separation. In that case, we will both suffer from a deterioration of neighborliness and be the victims of an indifference that could end in distrust and dislike.

There are other people who do not happen to live next door, or in the next apartment, or in the vicinity of my home. They are the ones whom I meet daily or almost daily. I work with them or for them, or they work for me. They are my colleagues or my students. They are the shop assistants, the bank manager, the man or woman at the desk, the many men and women and children with whom in the course of a day or week I have to do. What about my relationship with them?

Obviously in the large-scale planning of a business or a

school, we cannot think of each of them in his or her own personal integrity. In a way, they must be regarded as "objects"—but only *in a way*, since we all know (and experts in management are now proving this to be a demonstrable fact) that a condition for good industrial relations, to take one example, is genuine understanding of the employer and employee as more than "the management" and "the hands." Insofar as we have actual one-to-one contact with any or all of these, however, we can act toward them in the "I-you" way. And this is of quite enormous importance in the total human community.

It is neither possible nor necessary to try to spell out in detail the way in which this attitude will manifest itself. But we may give a few actual examples and make some comments that will indicate something of the right and sound way of relationship at this level. This is the best we can hope to provide in this discussion. Each of us has to work out for himself or herself just *what* is open to us in this or that situation. There is no standardized blueprint for social relationships.

When I am doing my shopping, how do I ask the assistance of, talk with, and regard the person who, as we say, is serving me? Here we have a pretty clear indication of our general attitude toward others with whom we are not intimate. The man or woman who is rude or indifferent to a shop assistant, for instance, has not yet learned to think of others as genuine human beings in the making. To such a person they are merely useful tools, a means to secure what is wanted at a particular moment. It is always possible, however, to show politeness, courtesy, and consideration. It is always possible to refrain from demanding too much from those who work for us. My mother used to tell me that she usually judged an acquaintance by the way in which she treated her servants. If she was considerate and courteous, she was a decent person; if she was rude and overdemanding, she was not. This applies as much to one's employees in a large business or plant as to those in domestic service. It also applies to those whose job it is to render some service to the public in a shop, office, or bank.

But more than politeness, courtesy, and consideration can be shown. There can also be a *kind* of friendliness. I am not referring here, of course, to the intimacy of friendship which we have with but a few people. Nor am I suggesting that we should attempt such genuine intimacy with others whom we meet casually. I have already said that this cannot be. I am saying only that it is perfectly possible to adopt a way of speaking and making requests that will not be arrogant, overbearing, inconsiderate, or domineering. Rather, it will be pleasant, perhaps slightly humorous, thoughtful of the other, cooperative, and cordial. As I write I think of a shop to which I go every day to make some small purchases. There are three or four young women who serve at the counter. Since the shop is in the center of town it is usually very busy throughout the day and the women who work there are hard put to keep up with the demands made by customers. The hours are long; the work, if not hard, is exacting; it must sometimes be an effort for them to be pleasant. How do the customers treat them? I have noticed some who come in, bark out an order, wait impatiently until it is filled, pay for it, leave without a smile or a word of thanks. They get what they want and that is that. The woman who served them might just as well have been a vending machine into which some coins were fed and from which the required article was obtained. Other customers, however, say good morning, ask for what they want, wait patiently, pay for their purchase, make some comment about the weather, smile, thank the assistant, and leave. I have noticed that it is these latter who awaken a response from the assistant.

She smiles in return, obviously she is pleased, and I have no doubt but that she likes the customers who treat her in this friendly fashion.

I have already quoted various remarks by the Anglo-American philosopher Whitehead. Now I quote something from his wife, Evelyn. In a report of conversations with Whitehead, Lucien Price (whose book will be mentioned later) quotes from time to time some remark or comment from her. In a discussion of American life as contrasted with life in England, she said, "I fell in love with this place when I came here to live; and where I love I'm not critical. But I do notice a hardness toward shop assistants by customers. It would be just as easy to be kinder when they haven't what one wants." This comment about *American* manners applies equally to those often found in Britain and elsewhere. Perhaps she had expected to find *more* consideration in America than in London, where she had lived. Her remark is open to a very wide interpretation, however. Is it not, in fact, just as easy to be decent to those with whom one is in contact, as it is to be inconsiderate or rude?

All that has been said on this subject is so obvious that it seems silly to put it down on paper. Yet I am convinced that the quality of human character is revealed in these little things that often may appear quite insignificant. The man or woman who has time for such courtesies is on the way to developing into the wholeness which includes living in the human community; he or she is really expressing human love in a fashion appropriate to the occasion. Thus this person can be seen as one who is growing toward the real meaning of being human —becoming more a lover-in-the-making. The man or woman who is not courteous or considerate in these seemingly tiny ways is often insecure in the inner life, terrified of exposing the self to others; hence she or he is moving in the direction of less fully human realization.

Possibly that person has been the victim of mistreatment by others that has warped his or her life; possibly he or she has refused, by repeated decisions, to be open to other people. At any rate, the end result is likely to be loss of inward vitality and an accompanying loss of relationships. Someone like that is a contradiction of the meaning of being human and a symbol of the rejection of the possibilities for shared life which humanity has within it.

What can be done for such tragic people? They can be accepted as they are, with no demands made upon them, beyond those which at the moment they can understand. They can be helped in various ways, but always without condescension. Perhaps the hard shell of their self-centered existence may be broken through. One never knows; one always hopes. It may be that through the courtesy and consideration, indeed the love, of others they will find themselves impelled, by no coercion but simply by the persuasive power of other people's interest and concern, to open up and let others into their life.

The classical account of the change which can be wrought is in Dickens' *A Christmas Carol.* The hard shell that Ebenezer Scrooge had used as a defense against any real contact with others was finally smashed by the sheer friendliness of others. The warmth that he had hidden, even tried to suppress, now had a chance to express itself. We need not be sentimental about this. It is always wrong to sentimentalize about people because thereby we fail to see them realistically and take them with sufficient seriousness. But without being sentimental, we *can* see that very often the basic difficulty with the hard, self-centered man or woman is to be traced to the simple fact that he or she has not known love from another or others and hence has never learned to love. Augustine spoke once of the "love which awakens love's response." When we *are* loved and *know* ourselves to be loved, we can begin to love back. This is why experts in child psychology are so insistent upon the necessity for affection shown to babies and small children. Only in this fashion, they tell us, can the young person begin to respond in a positive and affectionate way to other people.

In our increasingly mechanized and cybernetic culture personal relationships of the sort we have been discussing may become more difficult. A job on the assembly line in a large plant is hardly calculated to develop such relationships. All the more reason, then, to do everything in our power both to act in this fashion whenever and wherever possible and to work for conditions of work and life that will not entirely maim the human agents who must perform the mechanical tasks that sometimes seem so destructive of warmth, spontaneity, and open relationships with others.

The Italians have a word that they often use when they wish to ask for sympathetic understanding in a difficult situation or when they are faced with some seemingly impossible responsibility. It is *pazienza*. My small Italian dictionary gives its meaning as patience; but my larger one lists instances of its use which in context mean "try it out," "don't worry too much," "wait a little," "take it easy." To this I should add from my own knowledge of Italians, "be persevering," and "don't let this get you down." Like so many Italian words, its particular significance will be shown by inflection or intonation and by the gesture of the hands or the look on the face when it is said. *Pazienza* in all its senses is enormously needed in our contemporary society. It can help us face up to the pressures that we feel and perhaps find a way through the depersonalizing factors that so much affect our daily lives. Nowhere is *pazienza* more necessary than in the kind of relationships with which we are concerned in this chapter.

What it really comes down to, then, is that in our contacts with others we shall try to get on with them as human beings. We can do this only when and as we accept them as human beings and, with whatever degree of directness, set ourselves to help them to realize themselves as growing persons in the human community. I need not add that I am not suggesting a continual self-conscious awareness of what is going on. It is much more like a theme that runs beneath the whole of a movement in a symphony: not always obvious, yet, from time to time, vividly recalled in a given passage. The intentionality, as someone has phrased it, is always present, although it is not always in the forefront of our conscious minds. Psychologically that could not be the case, in any event. We must attend to other things as we go on with our daily activity. But yet it is there all the time, whether we are thinking about it or not. This is to say that we have become, or are on the way to becoming, the kind of persons who naturally and habitually think and act like that.

My reference to Italians a few paragraphs above provides the occasion to comment on the differences between races, nations, and even people, in respect to visible manifestation of this quality of openness in human relationships. The Latins are believed to be more "passionate," as we say; hence they express externally that which may be very difficult for an Anglo-Saxon to express at all. So, also, between this person and that person. Depending upon background, early training, previous decisions, and much else, someone will or will not be obviously expressive. There are vast differences in temperament, which we need to remember. Some find it much easier to show outwardly that which they feel deeply within them; others do not. This diversity is to be expected and welcomed: "it takes all sorts to make the world." There is no reason to think or want everyone to have the same way of indicating concern, care, and love.

But many of us are desperately in need of the "developed" heart that *can* express itself more readily. Training, family background, the old "class-consciousness" (now, happily, disappearing), and, perhaps above all, the experience of our early years in school, have had their disastrous consequences, as Forster saw. We are not cold; we are only undeveloped, so far as open, warm, and expressive behavior to others is concerned. Somehow we have been denied the help we needed to develop ways in which the warmth that is inside us can be communicated to those we meet.

I have just said, "above all the experiences of our early schooling." Perhaps nothing else has done more to make easy relationships, in genuine warmth, difficult if not impossible for many of us. Many of us, when young, heard so much about the "stiff upper lip" and have been warned so often against showing emotion. Thus we have become somewhat stilted, stern, and unyielding; and we find it extremely difficult to get into touch with others, save on superficial levels. This is why we have every reason to be grateful that, among younger people, a change is observable. The social structure has been altered; the school system has become liberalized; a more "continental" atmosphere has made itself felt. Older people are often shocked by the change. Perhaps it is good that they should be. The shock may force them to recognize the peril of self-destruction that their early training, under an older dispensation, brought so near. As a matter of fact, the newer spirit and attitude seem to me to mark the reemergence, after more than a century, of old "merry England" and its equivalents in other parts of the world.

Oddly enough, the Scots frequently appear to have escaped this danger, despite the common and mistaken notion that they are a "dour" people. Anyone who has spent much time in Scotland knows how wrong that idea is. The Scots have genuine warmth; and my opinion is that their quite different educational system has had a great deal to do with this. In the United States and

Canada, and in Australia and New Zealand too, where education has not been on such rigid lines, such warmth is also often found. But even in those lands, it is clear that people of an older generation who have attended independent schools modeled on the English system have something of the same difficulty with undeveloped hearts. Once again, however, the rigidity is giving way to a more genial and open attitude in educational institutions; and this is to be welcomed in those lands as much as it is in England.

While writing this chapter I have been obliged to leave my study in order to fulfill a professional responsibility. Walking along a street in Cambridge toward my college, I noticed once again the relaxation in dress and manners among the young people I passed. Their conversation with one another and their way of treating the young woman in the shop to which I went on my way to college were certainly easy and open. Somehow they seem to have learned the importance of freer expression, of kindness, and of accepting the principle of "live and let live." To me they seem more human, more likely to realize the potentialities of their humanity, more on the way to becoming whole, than the generation to which I belong. Alas, I was taught to be "manly," which often meant to suppress my deepest instincts and to refuse to allow the heart to develop.

I cite here a line that W.H. Auden wrote as World War II was breaking out: "We must love one another or die." In these words he stated a profound truth of which every one of us must take account. In their original context, the words were used to say that unless there is love (that is, sympathy, understanding, and concern) among us, the whole society to which we belong, and indeed any society that lacks these qualities, is headed for destruction. But the words apply with equal if not greater truth—and Auden was aware of this when he wrote them—to human relationship on the more personal level. I *must* love others or else *I* shall die. To me this is the simple truth about human existence.

The point here is not physical death, of course. Rather, it is the death of human selfhood. Here Auden is saying in a different way what Southwell said in the sentence I quoted earlier, "Not where I breathe, but where I love, I live." We are all going to die physically, whether this comes sooner or later. And it is essential that we acknowledge physical death and come to terms with it. A long time ago I heard a speaker startle his audience by saying, "The one certain fact about everyone who is within range of my voice is this: despite all the advances of medical science, he will soon be a corpse." We do die; and of that fact, with all its significance, we must be aware. Otherwise we are less than human. So far as we can see, the animals do not know that they are going to die; they have no awareness of what we call mortality. But we humans do have it as part of our distinctive human existence. It is not that, however, of which we are here speaking. For there are other deaths, worse deaths, than the physical one which awaits us. Their tragedy is in their happening not by natural necessity, but by our own decision.

We are dying as human beings when we are not moving in the direction of fulfillment. It may not seem to be death, but that is what it is. For it is failure to move toward true life, and its final end is destruction of potentiality, loss of human integrity, and the denial of our human meaning. A man or woman who is utterly and entirely self-centered, having no outlet for his or her energy toward others, unable or unwilling by a series of choices to enter into genuine contact, living only for individual interests, is on the way to death. Such a person is alive in a physical sense—apparently in good health, perhaps. Yet that man or woman is moribund, and sooner or later will become a living corpse.

116

True human life exists in relationships. So, I believe, does everything else in the universe. For us to become what we are meant to become, involves the development of those relationships so that they are ever more genuine, more marked by mutuality, more a matter of generous giving-and-receiving. This is what love signifies. Not to move in *that* direction is to move backward, so to say, toward nonbeing, nonentity, sheer nothingness. I recall hearing it said of an old teacher of mine, who at the time was well into his seventies, that he was always growing. Foolishly I commented, "By this time, I should have thought, he would already have grown all that he could." But I was wrong. *Nobody* reaches that stage. To grow, in the sense we are arguing here, *is* to be alive.

I once had an acquaintance who is to me a ghastly illustration of "living death" of this tragic kind. When I knew him reasonably well, so far as that was possible under the circumstances, he had evidently decided to withdraw into himself. He lived in such a way that he did not relate himself to others and made it impossible for them to relate to him. He was centered in himself and in his own interests—interests that were entirely good and sound but which received his attention simply because they were *his*. It would have been bad enough if all this had happened because of some defect in his background, but this was not the case: he came from a pleasant family, had received an excellent education, possessed sufficient means of support, and was of nice appearance. In fact, he had what young people call "everything going for him."

As I understood the situation, he had at one time exposed himself to another and had been much hurt by the treatment he received. But instead of accepting this, absorbing the sting of it, and going on from there a wiser and more understanding person (as many have become through just such an experience), he retreated into himself, closed and barred the door, and spent his time and effort in an increasingly narrow field of interest. He could have had some happiness in life; he could have given some happiness to others. But he had decided otherwise. He was *dead*, to all intents and purposes. Doubtless he would continue for years as a biological specimen; yet he was dead. And, in a sad sort of way, he must have been aware of the fact. For once, in a moment when his guard was down (thanks to his attending a party and drinking just enough to make him slightly, but not very, relaxed), someone heard him mutter, "Life is so lonely."

That was a revealing remark. His loneliness, which was not due to lack of physical contact with others in the sense of meeting them and, rather curtly, greeting them, was the sign of his inner deadness. He might have been able to cope with inner loneliness and hence become alive once again, had he been prepared to take the first steps toward others or respond to their approach to him. But he could, or would, do neither. Some of his acquaintances had tried their best to break through to him, but had failed. The doors were shut—indeed, usually the doors of his rooms were shut, too, so that it was very difficult to see him at all, save when he emerged to fulfill professional duties, or because of some necessary errand. I suppose that I have never seen anyone else so tragic or so impossible to assist.

I say that some had tried to break through to him. More than that, they had struggled very hard to do so. This effort was a testimony to their own deep humanity. For not only must we make ourselves available to others; we must do all in our power by that availability to deliver them from the possibility of the "living death" of not loving, not living in love. Readiness and willingness for this (as, when, and if it is possible to provide it), is a human privilege and responsibility. It is easier to act upon this principle in the more intimate areas of human relationship—with a member of one's own family, for example, who shows signs of retreat into the fortress of self, and fears an encounter with others. It is much more difficult in the area of the "I-you" type of human contact. Yet act upon it we must, both because the generosity of our spirit requires that we help others toward life and away from death, and also because our own movement toward wholeness depends upon just such readiness and willingness to help.

The amazing and marvelous thing is that in this way we can find great happiness. It is not directly sought, of course; it comes as a by-product of the satisfaction of our humanity found in sharing with others. To give ourselves to others, in whatever ways are open to us; to look for and find those ways when they are not immediately obvious, and to be ready to receive from others through the ways that they have discovered to reach us, is to be truly alive as human beings, to grow toward becoming human. If experience teaches anything, it teaches that. If we do love one another, in the various modes of loving possible for us, we are indeed alive. Our liveliness is also loveliness —which is to say that we unconsciously attract others because they have somehow seen love at work in our lives.

9

Being Part of the Human Race

THROUGHOUT THIS BOOK I have spoken often and emphatically about the social aspect of human existence. To live as human is to live in relationship and, above all, to realize that the love which is the clue to the meaning of being human requires such relationship with others. I have already discussed the lover, who is in deepest contact with others; life in the family, where intimate relationships between husband, wife, and children are nourished and strengthened; the friend, who is intimately related to those who share common interests and concerns and in whose companionship we find delight; and the neighbor or acquaintance whom we know in more general contact with other people. But there is still another area of human social relationship: each of us is part of the human race, belongs to the greater society of humankind, and is knit together in the common bundle of human life on this planet. A person who tries to live in total separation from that wider community of fellow humans would be attempting the impossible. None of us can escape sharing in the human lot.

I have just said that someone who tries to be completely

separate from the human race is attempting the impossible. Even if it could be done that person would, by that very fact, have ceased to be genuinely human. This must not be misunderstood. I am not contending that there should never be times when one is physically alone. A good deal of our human living is a matter of what Whitehead called solitariness; but he did not mean this in the ordinary sense of the word. He was talking about the need to have the time and opportunity to withdraw for a moment from the mob, to think things out, to ponder the human lot, and do all the other things that are best done when one is by oneself, as we often phrase it. But such solitariness is *not* the sort of separation which denies our common humanity; indeed it may be a condition for fuller participation in the common life. The sense of presence with and sharing in the life of others does not necessarily require constant physical proximity to them.

I am now writing these words in my study. Nobody else is here with me, in the physical sense. Nor has anyone been here with me for most of the day. That does not mean, however, that I am separated from my fellow men and women. If I am to continue writing this book I must for a time be away from other people in that physical sense or else I will be able to accomplish nothing. Yet others are very much present with me, although in a different way. I am thinking about them, about their nature and their needs, about what makes them human like myself. I bear with me, deep inside my very being, the ones for whom I care; they are inescapably with me wherever I may happen to be. To realize this it is not necessary to be able to see them at this moment with my outward vision nor hear them with my outward ears. We are all together as we are part of the human race, and we are deeply influenced by each other at every succeeding moment of our lives.

A husband is "with" his family although he may be on a

business trip in some distant city. He carries his family with him because in his very nature he is a family man. So, also, in other kinds of relationship. There is nothing mysterious about this; it is simply a matter of ordinary human experience of which we are all quite aware. Each of us was born into a particular family and, by that birth, was also born into the human family as a whole. That is our human situation, from which we cannot escape and from which we should not wish to escape.

When we add to this natural fact the truth that, in order to love—in order to be on the way to fulfilled selfhood—we need other people, the point is even more obvious. We need other people if we are to exist at all; we need them for the help they can give us in many different ways; we need them for companionship and comfort; we need them above all for their affection, their interest, and their concern for us. And they need us in equal measure. In a great variety of ways and with differing intensity and intimacy, we are making our contribution day by day to the human community; and that community is making our growth a possibility for us. We are all in this thing together. This *is* our situation. If we accept it and live in terms of it, we shall be on our way to greater wholeness and to the discovery of richer meaning in being human.

Stories have been told about a so-called wolf-child found in India some years ago. The stories are a little difficult to accept as they come to us; but apparently they have some basis in fact. They tell of a very young child, perhaps a tiny baby, who was kidnapped by wolves. The child lived with them, sharing their state and way of existence for some years. Later he was found and brought back to live again with humans. The stories say that by this time normal human development was impossible for him. Until his death a year or two later, he remained a wolf-child, although he managed to acquire a few human habits.

The accuracy of the details of these stories may be doubtful; but I am sure that the main point is plain and true enough. We may have human potentialities at birth but these cannot be developed in us without continuing contact with others of our human race. We are molded by them, at first quite unconsciously; we imitate them before we criticize them or try to differ from them. We learn from them something of the accumulated heritage of the human community. We are brought by them to share in the common life and to adopt the ways that this life has developed through the centuries. The specifically human environment brings out in us that which is hidden within us. This is not some purely automatic procedure; it is compounded of give-and-take, which includes our response to their activity toward us. There is a constant interplay of the growing self with the larger community of which that self is part, beginning with contact with parents and siblings and continuing with other men, women, and children until adolescence and eventual maturity.

"No man is an island, entire of itself," to repeat once more John Donne's famous words. Our sociality is integral to us; we are "part of the continent," as Donne says—part of the human race. What happens to *it* happens to us; what happens to us happens to it. If we were entirely encased in selfhood we might be an interesting type of animal but we should not be human.

One way in which we can come to realize the significance of our human sociality is by asking ourselves a simple question: "Where do *I* stop, and the world, and other people, begin?" Modern science has much to tell us of how we are organic to the natural order. We are part of it although we "emerge" from it. The chemical elements which make up our bodies are the same as those found in the natural world. (Indeed, some years ago a clever chemist said that it would be possible to evaluate a man or woman, chemically speaking, as worth about one American dollar! The same stuff could be purchased for use in a laboratory for about that price. Perhaps with inflation we are worth a little more nowadays!) These elements are arranged in certain patterns to produce living cells, permitting us to function in a distinctive way. But cellular structure like ours is present in those creatures we fondly call "lower" animals. We are not descendants of, but we are remote cousins to, the higher simians. So it goes. Nature influences us and we in our turn influence nature. Nowadays we recognize that our influence has been disastrous, as the present ecological crisis has demonstrated. In any event, we are part of the natural order and it is very hard to say just where *we* stop and that order, apart from us, has its beginning.

I shall not continue about this, however, although I believe that one aspect of human becoming of which we ought to be much more conscious is precisely this intimate relation to sticks and stones, stuff and dirt, the *things* which surround us. But that is not our present concern. Here I wish to go on to speak of the other half of the question posed above: "Where do I stop and other *people* begin?" Here, too, there can be no absolutely sharp separation. I know perfectly well that I am myself; but if I have any understanding of my situation I know also that I am so bound up with others in a common bundle of life that very often I sense that I am part of them and they of me.

Certainly there is a distinction between me and those others; but there is no complete separation. Here, once again, we have the difference already noted between the words distinction and separation. In this processive, interpenetrating world, there are no absolute separations, but there are genuine distinctions. While I am never identical with my friends, my family, my lover, my neighbors, my acquaintances, or anyone else, I never exist entirely apart from them. In the human community we remain each of us a self; at the same time we are always integrally part of that community.

Thus, our sociality is natural to us as humans, and it is increasingly clear that it is through our different sorts of relationships with others that we achieve whatever self-hood is ours, and are brought to a fuller realization of what it means to be human. Such relationships are *always* effective, regardless of what we think or do about them. This should not be taken to indicate that we are like drops of water whose identity is lost in the ocean. The meaning of our being human is attached not to some human mass but to this and that person, for *all* are able to realize in a personal and particular way that which they have in them to become.

To be conscious of our life in relationship is to be better equipped to handle it. What is more, our growth in love is dependent upon such a conscious recognition. As we are aware of another person, aware of our relationship with that other, and ready to act upon it in our own distinctive fashion, the situation as a whole becomes richer and much more likely to lead to our fulfillment in relational terms. At its most intensive, love is total; each lover lives in the other and both live in their love. This is much more than intellectual knowledge; it is emotional as well. It includes all the stuff of which we are made and brings the *whole* of us to greater integration.

An incidental comment is appropriate here. One of the characteristics of human beings is that they can think; that is, they are rational creatures. So I know *that* some-one else is there beside me. But knowing *that* someone is there is not identical with *knowing the person's very self.* Here intellectual awareness must be supplemented by sympathetic identification, not unlike the empathy of which writers on art speak when they wish to indicate genuine entrance into the reality of a painting, sculpture, poem, play, dance, or piece of music.

To return to our main theme, one of the dangers of modern Western people is to overemphasize what has come to be called individuality. We have already noted that an individual, by definition, is one instance of some given class, category, species, or type. In one sense we *are* that; but in a much deeper sense we are *persons*. The word person comes from Latin, where it originally meant either of two things: a legal entity about which judges and lawyers could talk (even today we speak of business concerns, universities, schools, and the like as "legal persons"), or the theatrical mask through which an actor spoke his part. The mask showed his role in the play and distinguished him from other actors.

This original use of the word has developed and changed during the centuries due to the increasing centering of interest on selfhood as a psychological process. The result is that, today, the word has come to mean a conscious focus of energies. But our contemporary experts in psychological investigation are not content with that. They insist more and more that person and society go together. Thus, when I suggest that we are persons much more than we are individuals, my point is that this self of mine, with its consciousness and self-consciousness, is by necessity influenced by, as it influences, other similar selves. This is why, in academic circles today, we hear so much about the intimate connection between personal psychology and social psychology. Without social belonging, we could not be persons. We should be individuals and that only.

Now I turn to a consideration of the types of social relationship. I need not speak of the family, or friendship, or neighborliness, or acquaintanceship, since these have already been discussed. Here our concern is with the large-scale social groups, which are just as much a part of our human existence, and some of them just as inevitable, as the more intimate ones. I am thinking of a whole series of these groups. There are trade unions, fraternal organizations, churches, and the like, that exist to bring together those who share some interest or support some common cause. In such groups the association is, for the most part, entirely voluntary. We do not *have* to belong; we *choose* to do so. But there are other groups which are involuntary: the village, town, or city, the nation of which I am willy-nilly a citizen. And finally there is the global community made up of all who live on this planet. Here I have no choice but to belong.

Each type of grouping is in its own way a manifestation of the total social belonging that is ours and is integral to our humanness. Some groups have particular goals or represent special interests; others have a broader significance. Yet all of them are ways of relationship with others; each of them provides opportunity for human beings to be together in some manner which helps them realize in concrete fact what it is to be human. Perhaps it may be useful to review the types of grouping I have noted and make a few comments about each of them.

I begin with the smaller and voluntary groups. We know how a dramatic club, to take one example, brings together people who wish to share a common interest: a liking and concern for the theater and stagecraft. A fraternal organization like the Masons, for example, offers relaxation with others and chance for entertainment, but chiefly an opportunity for charitable activities, mutual help in times of trouble, and burial benefits. Other clubs exist to provide a chance to play bridge, perhaps, or to attend the theater in a group, or to undertake some social work. Neighborhood associations give their attention to the betterment of the area and to participation in local government. All these are simply by way of illustration. They show that human beings enjoy association in the pursuit of special objectives that have been freely selected.

Slightly larger—and sometimes very much larger—groups may fall into the same general category. Trade unions will serve as an example. So also will nationwide or worldwide societies, like those for the protection of children or animals, those that look out for the aged or infirm, or (in an almost global fashion) the Red Cross and its parallel societies. Here, too, we must find place for the various Christian and non-Christian religious bodies. These are also voluntary, even in the countries that still retain so-called state churches. Today, membership in such state churches is merely nominal and does not indicate active participation. But it is perhaps significant that many people who might opt out prefer to remain "in"—very likely because they somehow sense a value in *belonging* to a religious group, even if this includes little actual practice. Whatever we may think about the value, or the truth or falsehood, of institutional embodiments of the religious dimension, these religious bodies in fact do bring together vast numbers of men and women in a common devotion to the faith that the group holds. The religious bodies, and many of the other groupings just listed, are especially important in associating people of both sexes, of different racial origins and backgrounds, of varying cultures and social classes, and of all ages. Thus they provide a wider opportunity for sharing than is offered in the smaller groups, which have but a single interest and attract a more restricted membership.

The voluntary associations have their value because membership in them is freely chosen. But there are two more types, in which such free decision is not possible. One is at the local and national level; the other is global.

Everyone lives in a particular place; by that simple fact everyone is a citizen of his village, town, or city. One cannot opt out of this citizenship, although one may be a good citizen or a bad one, may play some part in the affairs of the place or refuse to do so. Furthermore, one enjoys privileges from such citizenship: protection by police, the local fire brigade, and much else. Such privileges entail responsibilities, for one is bound to obey the local laws at the risk of punishment and one must pay local taxes.

One is also a citizen of the country in which one lives, enjoying, and paying taxes to support, the services and protection provided. One may be patriotic or one may not be. Usually one *is*, in some sense; for one will have a certain pride in the place where one lives and in the land of which it is a part. Culture and tradition make us so. Such patriotism can be generous; it can also be what Samuel Johnson styled "the last refuge of a scoundrel," serving as an excuse for bad behavior toward those considered foreigners and contempt for anything not familiar and expected.

Since every human being is by necessity part of such local and national communities, it is wise to be more than a nominal citizen. Naturally one will try to be law-abiding, save when the laws outrage one's conscience. But more than that is likely. There can be concern with politics; interest in movements for the improvement of local or national life, or familiarity with history, which enables one to enter into the past that has made the present-day community possible. Surprisingly enough, as the reader may think, all this is a kind of love. Despite Dr. Johnson's saying, probably few things are less harmful and more likely to enhance life than a sincere but not uncritical love of one's town and one's native (or adopted) country.

Within the national life there are other groupings: employers and employees for example. These may pose problems from time to time, but they are not nearly as dangerous as the question of race. When two or three different races happen to live together in a given country, there is always the possibility of antagonism and conflict. The reasons for this are found in differing temperaments and outlooks. But there is also the strange fear, found in so many otherwise intelligent people, of those whose color is different from their own. When racial antipathy is strong, a serious situation can develop. We have seen this in our own time in South Africa, in the United States, and elsewhere—even in Britain, which has had a long history of racial toleration. At its worst, this may bring about the ghastly spectacle of segregation by law, apartheid; when it does not reach that extreme it can show itself in denial of equality in ways big or little. Worst of all, it can be expressed in the refusal to express affection and concern for those of another race or color.

The truth is, of course, that racial diversity is a good thing. Arnold Toynbee has written in *The Study of History* about the great contribution the black race has made to American culture. But apart from any such contribution, we are all members of the human race and all should be treated as such. Equality of opportunity, full civil rights, and freedom to make to the common life whatever distinctive contribution is possible are natural expectations and should be accorded to all, regardless of race or color.

The second type of association that we all must accept as a given fact is what I have called the global aspect of human life. Within recent times, thanks to travel, exploration, opening of trade possibilities, and many other factors, the reality of this global belonging has been brought home to us in a striking manner. During World War II, the American statesman Wendell Willkie coined the phrase, "ours is one world." It is indeed one world; and whether we are Englishmen or Americans, Russians or Chinese, Italians or Indians, we all belong to it. Circumstances now force us to recognize that all men and women belong together, whatever their nationality, race, education, class, religion, or culture. We belong together because we live together on this planet, which seems to grow ever smaller as more effective and rapid means of communication are developed. Furthermore, the pressure of events, along with economic and political realities, make us more and more interdependent. World citizenship is now a palpable truth, not just an abstract idea.

I trust that the reason for these comments is apparent. I have wished to show that human beings are by nature as well as inclination in and of the total human community. They need such sharing; and whether they like it or not, they must accept it as a fact. Family and friends, acquaintances and neighbors, yes; voluntary membership in voluntary associations, yes; but also the necessary and inescapable belonging to place and nation, and above all to the world community—these in varying ways provide us with the social environment that contributes so largely and necessarily to our human growth. They are all ways in which the reality of comradeship is established and given. In joy and sorrow, in need felt and help given, in every area and aspect of human experience, none of us is entirely alone. The ancient Hebrew scriptures depict God as saying, "It is not good for man to be alone"; therefore God is said to have established the family. We may take this as a symbol of the truth that in the grain of the universe there is some movement toward togetherness. Nothing can destroy it; it is there as a fact. Robert Frost's familiar poem "Mending Wall" puts it clearly when it speaks of something which does not like a wall and hence which wants it *down*. We cannot live in separation or isolation.

Yet human community, on whatever scale, is healthy only when it is centered in the meaning and value of those who belong. Otherwise it can be an impediment to true development; it can damage our true human growth. This is why self-regarding societies are often so dangerous.

The purposes that any group serves must be *good* purposes, purposes that can be shared without harm to those who belong to the group. We can think of a society of crooks or thieves or bandits, who live by preying on other people. There are such groups of people, to be sure; but their ends are socially negative and harmful. Such a criminal association provides a sense of community to those who are its members, but because its aim is antisocial and its goals destructive of the integrity of others, it is an evil thing. Not only is it a cancer in the healthy organism of humanity as a whole; it is also bad for those who belong to that group, although they may not be aware of this sad truth. It is bad for them because it fails to promote the development of their human potentialities in the right direction. On the contrary, it promotes such development in the wrong one, where genuine human sociality becomes less possible and its integrity is continually threatened.

This suggests to us the need for a continuing purification of the motives and methods of any social group. Anything that narrows, restricts, negates, or denies the fullest realization of self in community, is by that token evil. It is evil because it is a barrier to the living in love which is our human purpose and meaning. A whole nation, for example, can be caught up in such evil. We witnessed this in the case of Nazi Germany, destructive as it was of human integrity at every level of national and global existence.

If we had space, it would have been desirable at this point to speak once again at length about that other aspect of our belonging: I refer to our belonging to the natural environment, upon which we live, from which we are supported, and for which (as fortunately we are now coming to see) we have responsibility. But the brief comment in an earlier part of this chapter must suffice to indicate that I am very conscious of this whole area.

Above all I should emphasize the peril present in what Bertrand Russell once called "cosmic impiety," by which he meant an attitude toward life that, in its rightful stress on *human* affairs, fails to take sufficiently into account humanity's larger setting in the natural order.

It is with that *human* situation, however, that we are concerning ourselves in this book, although in the last chapter a good deal must be said about what our human living may imply about the deeper cosmic situation. I hope that I have shown the necessity laid upon each of us to come to grips with the sociality that is the setting for, and the condition of, our personal development in realizing the meaning of being human. Once more I emphasize *relationship*. Our world (including the natural order) is a world of relationship. Nothing exists in and of itself, as what philosophers would call a "discrete" (or entirely isolable) entity; everything is related to its environment. When Teilhard de Chardin said that, in such a world, the end increasingly in view is "amorization," or growth in love, he was speaking nothing but the truth. For love *is* the basic significance of relationships, when they are healthy and right, harmonious and good. In the last analysis, all the social groupings about which we have spoken have their value in their capacity to provide for us the opportunity to grow in love.

10

Growing Old Gracefully

I CAN SPEAK with some authority about growing old since I am now doing that myself. When one is seventy-five and more, naturally one begins to think about the matter. And the material for one's thought is largely provided by one's own experience and feelings, rather than by more abstract considerations. One knows what growing old is like; one knows this firsthand and not by the reports of others. One hopes that one can face advancing age, with its problems and its opportunities, in a graceful way. Few things are more unpleasant to see than a man or woman who grows old *dis*-gracefully, in resentment and bitterness, complaining and protesting, hating each new day and lamenting the inevitable slowing down, the loss of physical energy, and the restriction of activity which old age imposes.

Growing old is a fact. It happens to everyone. Even the youngest of us is growing *older*, which is often forgotten. In an earlier time somebody who had reached forty years was considered an old man or woman, or at least to have entered upon old age; today we should say that such a person is barely middle-aged. Medical advance has done much to lengthen the span of life, and nowadays we expect to live at least the traditional "three-score years and ten," if not longer. But whether early or late, old age will come. It is absurd to resent what is inevitable. We should learn to accept it and make the best we can of it.

I spoke above of the loss of physical energy that accompanies our growing old. That is an unquestioned fact. But it is by no means always the case that intellectual and emotional energy decrease when a man or woman has passed beyond the early sixties and is beginning to recognize that he or she is growing old. Indeed, there is a considerable number of men and women whose intellectual capacity seems to be intensified with increasing age, and many of us must have known some whose emotional response was very strong. In both of these ways, it may very well be that we have a natural compensation for the diminishing physical energy to do what once was possible. In this sense, a human being is as old as he or she feels and thinks. Some who are ripe in years are young in mind, spirit, and feeling. Total decrepitude is not a necessary condition of old age.

As I write, I recall a man who for many years was very close to me, as the head of the college in which I taught and lived. He had continued in his post beyond the usual retirement age, in order to see the college through World War II and the subsequent year or two of adjustment to the postwar situation. He was in his early seventies when finally he gave up work. He had never been in robust health, although he had carried an enormous burden of responsibility without apparent ill effects. After retirement he lived for ten years. Throughout his life he had been one of those remarkable people who never lose their intellectual curiosity, their zest for life, and their interest in all that is going on around them. Some of us who loved him dearly feared that with retirement he might begin "going down hill" in these respects. But we need not have worried, since far from doing this he seemed even more eager and alive, curious and interested; his zest for life was increased. I saw him frequently; and his conversation was as bright and sparkling as ever, while his reading continued unabated and his critical powers never failed. Shortly before his death I spent the greater part of a day with him. He talked about a book he had just read and I was astounded that a man of more than eighty was still able to make penetrating critical comments, to appreciate a good style of writing, and to use the book as the starting place for some observations of his own, which were as keen as ever. During the three weeks of his final illness I visited him almost every day in hospital. Until the very end, when his mind was clouded because of heavy medication to ease severe pain, the same eagerness and alertness, curiosity and zest, were with him. He was interested in his nurses and pleasant to them whenever they did something for him, he welcomed visitors to his sickroom, he talked with them, even when he was in pain, as he had done in the old days. In fact, some of us remarked afterward that it was he, not we, who seemed most alive in conversation.

This man whom I knew so well and loved so dearly was by no means unique. Most of us have known others very much like him. He and they had learned how to grow old in a graceful way. They had learned that they must accept physical infirmity and must "go slow," but they had not allowed this restriction to produce in them mental, emotional, or spiritual inertia. As they drew nearer to death, they seemed to be ever more alive.

The first thing to notice, then, is that growth toward wholeness is not brought to a stop by increasing age—or it *need* not be. There is no reason to think that the process of becoming human comes to an end at some particular age. On the contrary, there is every reason to think that it is a lifelong movement that continues all our days, that does not stop at the end of some given number of years. To be human, as I have said, is to be on the way to becoming more human; and people like this are outstanding examples of what it means to be human in this sense. They also show that in this process of becoming, deep relationships with others are entirely possible although, naturally, the ways in which response is made in these relationships differs from those found in earlier years.

Second, we should observe that for most of us this capacity to continue in the direction of wholeness, with openness to others, must be cultivated. One of the ways to prepare ourselves for old age is by starting this cultivation long before we begin to feel our age. It will be almost, but not entirely, impossible to acquire this quality when one has gone into retirement from active work. We need to put ourselves in the way of it long before that time.

The capacity to be open or available to others, once it has been cultivated, provides part of the genuine happiness of old age. But other persons must be available too: here the older person may find a difficulty. In youth it is easy to make friends and there is great opportunity to meet people and to know them reasonably well. But later on, this is not often such a simple matter. Older people seem to have a built-in fear that they are not wanted by others, especially by those who are much younger. This fear is, I think, mistaken. The truth of the matter is that younger people are shy about intruding themselves on their elders. They feel a little embarrassment about making the first step. And this is where the older person can help. Often it is up to him or her to take that first step and to let the younger ones know that there is a welcome for their companionship and friendship. Once this is done, the response can sometimes be overwhelming, as I know from my own experience.

It is enormously important, then—and this is my third point—for those of us who are in advanced middle-age or approaching old age, as well as for those of us who are already old, to cultivate friendship with other people; and, I should say, to attempt this especially with those who are younger. Of course, there are times when a man in his seventies or beyond feels more comfortable with others of his own age. The reasons for this are obvious. There are similarities of interests, perhaps; certainly there are memories that can be meaningfully shared with others who have had much the same sort of experience. But there are also times when such people wish to get in touch with new ideas and contemporary ways of seeing things, and to learn what is going on in a world that they themselves have not known intimately and at firsthand. It is better, therefore, not to try to confine one's friendships to one's own contemporaries. The way to keep alive and alert, and to retain zest, is by sharing the approach, attitudes, and interests of those whose perspective is *not* one's own, who belong to a different age group, and who can bring tidings of a different sort of world from the one in which the older person has spent most of his or her days. Moreover, the younger person can also be enriched. Take, for example, a close friendship between a man in his middle seventies and another in his early forties—to speak from one such friendship known to me. The older man has learned much in the way of new ideas and beliefs, while the younger has picked up something from the experience of his friend. Both have profited from the relationship; both have been helped to grow toward their proper wholeness.

Again, it is good for older persons to have some particular interest that can occupy their time and provide continuing activity. I have already spoken about hobbies; and this is the sort of thing I have in mind here. I am thinking of some subject of reading and study, some craft, indeed, some "anything," that will be properly time-consuming and able to absorb the interest of the one who engages in it. One of the problems in old age is simply that there is so much time. This may seem highly paradoxical since in fact there is so little time. My meaning is that before retirement from active work much of the day was devoted to doing the job in which one was employed; but after retirement, there are all the hours of the day with nothing to do unless some activity is found. Anyone who is growing old knows that this is the case. What will he or she do with the time that is now on hand? If one has learned somehow to interest oneself in what may have been, earlier on, a part-time activity, one can now give oneself to it in a more concentrated fashion. It can become a nearly full-time activity. One has the leisure to make this possible.

I have two acquaintances whose experience is illuminating. One of them, a highly educated person, found what he called his "salvation" in old age by turning to the plays of Shakespeare. He had always been interested in those plays but had never had the opportunity to study them carefully. When he retired he first familiarized himself with the texts, then studied them in their historical setting, traced their development of themes, and informed himself about different interpretations of them. He was not a professional literary scholar and made no pretense to expert knowledge. But this interest, which had started before retirement when he had happened one year to see three productions of *Hamlet* with three different leading actors, was for him a consuming passion. Not only did it provide him with something that occupied his time, although this was important in itself; it also made him a most interesting person to be with, since he could talk so knowledgeably, yet not tediously, to anyone who wished to discuss Shakespeare.

The other acquaintance was not sophisticated in any way. She had worked for years in a very minor post in an office. Her hobby had been pottery. It was wonderful for her when she could give all her time to this activity.

Again, she was no expert; at best she was a talented amateur. The things she made seemed lovely to some of us, but she said that they were really only second-rate. However that may be, she had something which took her time and provided her with an interest that gave her great joy for as long as she lived.

Older persons who are in this situation may count themselves blessed. Any of us can find some interest to provide for our days of enforced "doing nothing," when we are relieved of our earlier responsibilities in work. I personally have found that in these days when my duties are less exacting—although I have not fully retired from my teaching and my supervision of research students—a careful study of my philosophical master Whitehead, begun many years ago, has given me the greatest pleasure and happily filled the long hours when I might very well have been wasting my time with no specific interest to keep me happy.

Still another way of using time profitably when age comes is visiting the sick, offering oneself for collecting funds for some useful purpose, and even the humdrum business of baby-sitting. The list could be continued almost indefinitely, of course, but these may be suggestive. Many of my older friends gladly engage in one or more of them from time to time. They tell me that their recompense is the feeling that they are rendering needed assistance that younger and busier people cannot easily give.

Once again I recall a man I once knew well. He is an illustration of the danger that arises when an older person does *not* have some interest to occupy his time and attention. He was in his early eighties when he died. He had lived his entire life in his college, of which at one time he had been the head. He had enormous charm, his colleagues were kind to him, and with some few of the junior members he was able to be friendly and companionable. But because of age he could not do the many things to which he had been accustomed. He could not travel as he had liked. It was even difficult for him to get around easily in the town. Most of the time he sat in his own rooms or in the "combination" room of the college, doing nothing but moping. He was miserable. With him I contrast another man, one of his colleagues, a man only two or three years younger. This retired don also lived in his college. He was outgoing, interested, eager to meet new people, delighted when he could see an old student or entertain a guest. His presence was welcomed everywhere. Even when he repeated stories that many of us had heard a hundred times, he did it with such verve that nobody could object to the repetition. When he died, he was full of years but beloved by the whole society. His colleagues felt they had lost a genuine friend; the juniors knew that they had lost a valued counselor to whom they had always been able to turn.

The difference between the two was that the former had never developed any special interests beyond his academic one; hence, when he could no longer lecture and supervise, he was lost. The latter had never permitted himself to be so much on one track; he had a wide variety of interests, the special one being Greek tragedy. Indeed, on the evening before his quite sudden death he had entertained in his rooms a group of senior and junior members who had read together one of Sophocles' plays. He had grown old gracefully; his friend had not.

I come now to the next, and in some ways most important, possibility offered by old age. My way of phrasing it was suggested to me many years ago by an uncle who was in his late seventies. We were talking one day about the amount of time that he had for doing what he called "just thinking." And he said, "One of the things I've been able to do these days is to make a treaty of peace with life."

During our workaday years we may very well be so immersed in our work that we have little, if any, time "just to think." Yet thinking is part of what it means to be human, although it is by no means all that being human signifies. Even professional scholars find that they have insufficient time to think outside the area of their immediate concern. I myself am well aware of this fact. My special subject requires me to think; but the sort of thinking it demands is along quite definite and narrow lines. I have pursued these lines the whole of my life. Only when I was relieved of some of my usual duties and hence had much more freedom than before, did I find opportunity to do that which I have been trying to do in the writing of this book. That is, to think long and hard about what being human means. Naturally I had had notions on the subject, glimpses here and there; but I had not given the subject the concentrated attention it deserves. And now, in doing just this, I have indeed found myself coming to the point where I have made "a treaty of peace with life." I am not at all unusual here. In different ways, from different approaches, out of different kinds of experience, any man or woman who is growing older can and should do something of the sort.

I do not wish to give the impression, however, that old age is a time for serious things only. Play and amusement have their place too. Special interests provide the aging person with some of the amusement that is needed. But there can also be other kinds of amusement; one can play, even if what one plays *at* is no longer so active as youth permitted. Theater, films, radio, television, reading, such travel as is possible, hours spent with old and new friends, games of cards—there are so many things open to an older person that it is impossible to suggest more than a few.

But I return to my insistence that one of the very best things for an older person is to be with younger folk. Doubtless, under present conditions, with smaller houses and differing social customs, it is necessary for many men and women who have reached fairly advanced years to go

142

to a home for people of their age. This has advantages, but it has disadvantages too. Those who reside in such establishments are often deprived of contact with new ideas, new customs, new perspectives; and this can be unfortunate for them. Yet, even there, it is always possible to make friends, including younger visitors—and that is what matters most of all.

Those persons may count themselves happy who discover, as they grow older, that at least one person in particular loves them dearly. For a husband and wife, there is the joy of growing old together, still in love with each other and delighting in that fact. They can find each other even better companions than in the days when they spent most of their time at work. Children and grandchildren enter the picture and they can provide genuine affection. But sometimes the person who dearly loves an older man or woman is not a relative at all. It is someone who may have been an acquaintance during the earlier course of life and with whom now is found a much closer relationship. In older people there is often an enormous capacity to love and a readiness to receive love from another. Such love is enjoyed for its own sake; but it has the additional value, in old age, of giving a certain security that might otherwise be lacking. And this is important for an older person.

It is perhaps best of all if the one who loves an older person is somewhat younger. There can be a depth of sharing which is often surprising. The relationship is tinged with a certain sadness, to be sure, since obviously it cannot last for a long time in terms of mortal years. That very fact, however, can make it a more generous relationship on both sides. The younger friend can help the older in many different ways, without ever obtruding that help. The older can give from experience the equally unobtrusive counsel which younger people often want but do not like to request. Both can grow in humanness, realizing their potentiality as human beings who give and receive.

There can be tenderness, gentleness, mutual concern, all of which are summed up in the word love. For an older man or woman, this can be positively redemptive.

The danger here is possessiveness on the part of the older partner. We can readily understand how this may come about. The dependence is greater, the need for companionship more intense. For this reason the older one needs to be very careful to see that the younger friend is allowed to "be." If there is true love, it cannot coerce or force; neither can it seek to possess. That means that one must be on guard against demanding too much time and attention from the other. Nor can one "use" the other and exploit him or her for one's own ends. That, too, would be a denial of love. The condition of this relationship, in its full beauty and worth, is freedom on both sides, with acceptance of each by the other *as* he or she is, *for what* he or she is, and with awareness of what he or she *may become*.

Knowledge that another cares, and cares deeply, enables the older person to put up with the pain, suffering, and occasional loneliness, which, along with diminishing physical energy, are associated with old age. And when the last illness comes and death is near, such a person can accept that, too, because there has been the discovery that there is something eternal in true love, whether one is, or is not, prepared to think of that eternal quality in terms of what is commonly styled "the future life." The love is here and now. But it also seems to have a dimension that is beyond this here and now. Nothing can destroy the reality of the love as a given fact, as something which has been known, shared, enjoyed, and suffered by those who have loved each other. There may be *more* than that, too, since mutuality and tenderness, with all these mean, seem to demand that even beyond death love shall somehow persist. But that could be only a hope, not a certainty —although we must recognize that the hope may be strong, vigorous, eager, and all-expectant, being grounded in a present experience which in itself is supremely good.

Very often a man or woman who is growing old fears that sexuality will disappear or at least very greatly diminish. He or she may even have been warned that this will happen; and, naturally, there is dread of the possibility that something so enriching in the drive to self-realization will no longer be part of life. If this should take place, it may seem that much of the color and vividness of being human will have gone too.

But in recent years, experts in sexual matters have told us that this fear is quite groundless. They have proved from the study of actual cases that the great majority of older people, sometimes at a very advanced age, not only continue to experience sexual desire but also can and do act upon that desire. Some of these experts have even said that a characteristic of older people may be an intensification of the sexual instinct. Of course, the frequency of physical expression may be less and its manner may be somewhat different, at least in some instances. But its reality is still present; and it can be very strong. I wish to emphasize this point because I have known so many who have felt that fear and who are deeply troubled at what they have come to believe is the certainty that something so central to human growth, so integral to human movement toward wholeness, will be denied them altogether.

The point is, of course, that older people are still human; that human existence is always based in part upon physiological and psychological sexual factors; and that human love is itself intimately related to all this. We have seen that this is no matter for shame; it is simply a matter of fact. We have also seen that sexuality may be expressed in different ways, appropriate to particular people and particular circumstances. For those who marry or are in a union of another sort, there is one way, in specific genital contact; for friends there is another way. Even in neighborly relationships, this sexual basis is present. In truth, as I have stressed, sexuality in this broader sense pervades all life. Here Freud was entirely right; and centuries ago the African Christian thinker Augustine understood and said the same thing, even if in his case it was eventually accompanied by a jaundiced distrust of natural human sexuality. Nor can we forget the homosexual expression of love, with or without physical contacts. In all of these ways, to be human is to be sexual. Old men and old women, because they are human, are sexual. It is not surprising that their sexual instinct, desire, and drive can continue.

It is to be regretted that very occasionally an older person may seek some extravagant and socially improper way to express this desire that is still so much part of life. But such instances are very infrequent; there are far fewer "dirty old men" and "dirty old women" than popular newspaper reports would suggest. Further, if they have been helped to see the reality and presence of sexuality and have not been led to think that, in old age, it is either absent or to be entirely suppressed, they probably would not behave in unacceptable ways.

We are at the end of our discussion on growing old gracefully. I wish to conclude by singling out that adverb *gracefully*. What is its meaning? In our Western tradition the word grace has been used to denote both the favor and the power of God, given to us. The word also carries the connotation of attractiveness, beauty, positive goodness, loveliness, even charm. Something of each of these has been in my mind as I have written this chapter. I have been thinking of the way in which all human life is, from one point of view, a matter of grace. I am not talking now of the specifically religious significance that it has had in Western culture. I am referring to the simple truth that we grow in selfhood as we are surrounded by favor, help, assistance, and acceptance, and as we are strengthened and ennobled by the many influences that have had their effect upon us. Any honest person recognizes that he or she has received much more than has been earned. Life has been a gift. So have wife, husband, lover, friends, even the world of nature that is our environment. *We* did not create them nor did we pay in cash for the right to enjoy them. Thus we may say that to live gracefully is to live as one who gladly and humbly receives much, very much indeed, as a gift, to which one will respond as best one can. In that sense, graceful living is simply the readiness to accept the grace which is given us, to be thankful for it, and to be the sort of person through whom such grace may also flow out to affect and assist others.

Perhaps older people are more keenly aware than younger ones of the extent to which life is a gift. A very old friend of mine once said to me, "Every evening I am thankful that I have been given another day; every morning I am thankful that still one more day is before me." To be able to say that, and mean it, is to grow old gracefully.

These few comments on grace bring us to the threshold of still another matter of importance. There is a question that older people (but not only they, since younger ones may feel it even more strongly from time to time) must ask themselves: "What is the *point* of human living?" Its meaning is self-fulfillment in human existence, realizing human potentialities, becoming whole, moving in the direction of genuine personhood shared in community. The clue to that deep meaning is in relationship in love. Is this ultimately frustrated, without any enduring value or permanent worth in the structure of things? Or, is it so deeply grounded in that structure that, come what may, we are still able to trust it, live in terms of it, and die in confidence that it is not an illusion?

This is the question that remains to be considered.

11

The Point of It All

FIRST OF ALL, let me summarize what has been said in the preceding chapters so that we will be better prepared to face the question: What is the point of it all?

We have found the meaning of being human to lie in growth in potentiality so that wholeness is achieved. This is always in relationship with others, since each of us is a social being requiring the presence and help of his or her fellows to develop in the right direction. But all relationship is a sharing that may become love; and love is the clue to human meaning. Decisions, made in such freedom as is ours, provide the way in which the movement to fullness takes place; and the best decisions are decisions made in love for that which can be shared together.

I have stressed the human capacity to love and explored at some length the significance of this central experience, its basis in physiological-psychological sexuality, and its expression in the family, in union of lives, in friendship, and in neighborly relations and the wider human community. Finally, I spoke of how it is possible to grow old gracefully, in gratitude for the gift of life and the many influences for good that have made our human becoming both possible and actual.

Throughout, my concern has been to stress that we learn what life is all about by the business of living it; and that the best interpretation is in terms of the love that is mutuality, giving-and-receiving, tenderness, and understanding. So, as in the words of Kirsopp Lake, we must live by a kind of faith; but that faith is "not belief in spite of evidence, but life in scorn of consequence."

So we come to the question: What is the point of it all? Or, as we phrased it at the end of the last chapter: Is this human existence, which finds its meaning in shared love, nothing other than an illusion, good enough for the present moment but without any permanent status in the universe? Or, is it somehow related to that universe in such a way that life can be lived "in scorn of consequence"?

Let us recall, first of all, how those who are living in love have the feeling that they are also living "in love"—if I again may play a little with words. I mean that, in the experience of love (and more especially in the deep and intimate love of husband and wife or lover and beloved), there is a sense of somehow going along with "the grain of the universe." We also noted that people who know such deep and intimate love feel that this reality of love is greater than either of them, greater also than both of them together. Thus they have an awareness, usually never articulated, that the love which knits them together is not only *theirs* but, in some mysterious fashion, is theirs because it has been given them and permitted for them to enjoy.

Is this awareness or feeling illusory? Is it simply a matter of human emotion? Doubtless it could be interpreted as the latter; but to me this would seem to be a concession to skepticism, entirely unnecessary and in itself a mistaken attitude to life, an instance of the "nothing-but" fallacy. I believe that this awareness or feeling points to a truth, however we may decide to interpret the truth to which it points. For the most part, I believe, it is wise to trust our simple but profound feelings as indicative of something that is genuinely *there*. What we have here to trust is an intuition, a hint, about how things go in the world, in spite of everything that may seem to argue against their going that way.

None of us can hope to understand "the scheme of things entire," in Omar Khayyám's phrase. To claim that we have done so is absurd on the face of it. Our human knowledge is tiny compared to the vastness of the universe. As Isaac Newton said, we are like children gathering pebbles on the seashore, with the enormous stretch of the ocean before us. Even if we knew more, we should not necessarily understand more. Our human capacity for understanding, like our knowledge, is finite and limited. Let us grant this. But at the same time, there can be no question that men and women have always felt that in the experience of love they are given some glimpse of what is deepest in the structure, and strongest in the dynamic, of this vast, mysterious, and largely inexplicable world. Matthew Arnold, writing in "Dover Beach" about the apparent defeat of all human aspiration, says that at least we have our love, and we can trust that. Arnold thinks, evidently, that this trust is not indicative of anything beyond itself, or if it is, the indication is not obvious. But those who love and who feel themselves "in love" cannot rest content with that. They not only want, but they feel that they find, a cosmic setting for their love. This is why they can make their own the words of Thornton Wilder, "Love [is] the only survival, the only meaning."

Now it is at this point that we are led to think about the religious dimension in human living. I have not yet spoken much about this and have postponed the matter for a good reason. The word religion is highly ambiguous; it can mean a great number of different things, some of them bad, some of them good, some of them half bad and half good. It seemed best not to complicate our consideration of the meaning of being human by introducing such an ambiguous word until the time had come when it might be brought into the picture in its right and sound sense.

First, let us honestly admit that much of what the antireligious have to say on the subject is correct enough. Some people mean by religion the absurd pretension that they know almost everything about everything; they think that they are able to draw a precise chart of heaven and earth and to say that the chart is final and complete. People like that diminish the mystery of the world and of human existence in that world. Others act as if religion gives them a right to claim special privileges, as those to whom has been revealed enough to put them in a category superior to their fellows. They are the "chosen" ones; the rest of us are beyond the pale. With yet others, religion means a concern for individual salvation from a troubled and troublesome world; it has been a method of extrication from the changes and chances of life here and now—an escape from reality. Unfortunately, religion is often identified with an unthinking conservatism that refuses to recognize the fact of change and the necessity for adaptation to change.

Nonetheless, religion in its best sense points to some persistent awareness, found in sophisticated intellectuals as well as in primitive savages, that there is something in the universe that is much greater than humanity, greater than any single man or woman or the whole human race, greater even than the totality of nature; and that this something expresses itself in the created order and in human life in different ways but always in order to intensify the richness and worth of what is happening in the world. Both primitives and sophisticates have been sure that we must adjust ourselves to that something, relate ourselves with it, respond to it, and work in cooperation with its purpose if human existence is to have ultimate value.

This positive aspect of the religious dimension has had its representatives in the great masters, teachers, prophets, and seers of what scholars call "the high religions," such as Hinduism, Buddhism, Judaism, Islam, and Christianity. Of course, these religions have often fallen victim to narrowness, pretension, superstition, and escapism. But this is not the whole story. They seem to have had in themselves a capacity to recover and to stress once again the insights of their founders or great teachers. Many of the most truly human, completely integrated, noblest, and wisest men and women have been devout believers in one or other of them; and simple people, living their daily humdrum lives, have found in them inspiration, courage, consolation, and strength. The great leaders who have founded such religions, or upon whose teaching and action such religions have been built, have been the most effective agents in human history. Gautama Buddha, Moses, Muhammad, Zoroaster, Isaiah and Jeremiah, and Jesus of Nazareth are not to be dismissed as irrelevant, nor can their teaching be regarded as insignificant. There is something there, in what they have said and done, that has mattered enormously and still does matter for millions of people. We must reckon with it.

The fascinating fact is that these men and others like them have been moving toward an insistence on the absolute centrality of relationship in human life, and within that context, on the centrality of love. Religions may have postulated a barbarous deity in early times; but the direction has consistently been toward playing down that coercive side and putting the stress on tenderness, gentleness, pity, identification with the world, and sheer goodness and righteousness as the essential characteristics of the divine. When this insight has been combined, as often it has, with other notions that seem to contradict it, it yet rings through, and with increasing clarity as the historical development proceeds. The emphasis on love is heard dimly at first, then more plainly, until it comes to vivid clarity in the teaching and life of Jesus. Even before him, in a spiritual master like the Buddha, profound compassion is seen to be the great motif, despite the metaphysical negations, the ascetic denials, and the dismissal of the value of personhood in what has come down to us as his teaching. Again, the intuition of a cosmic righteousness that seeks the good and finally emerges as parental love is present in the Jewish prophets, in spite of the sometimes ruthless moralism and often imperialistic conception of deity that run through their teaching. Supremely in Jesus, both in his teaching and in his life, love is exhibited as the secret of life and of the world where life is lived.

Only a very illiberal mind would disregard this persistent strain in the great religions. Only a very superficial spirit would refuse to take with utmost seriousness what these great masters believed they had discerned. Both common sense and human feeling tell us that their insight was and is of the highest importance. We had better attend to them and to their words.

The reader will understand, of course, that in this chapter I am not intending to convert anybody to anything, save to the reality of love and its sheer necessity if human life is to be more than a mere bagatelle. But it is my conviction that an instructed and open-minded man or woman owes it to himself or herself to consider this matter of deep religion. Only so can one show a genuine concern for honest and fair evaluation, for truth rather than for one's own fancies or preferences.

The best thing for me to do is to write personally, out of

my own experience and in the light of the faith which has grown in me over the years, accompanied as this has been by considerable anguish and suffering: for on such matters, personal reflection and witness cannot be avoided. Nonetheless the intuition that love is both human and cosmic in its sweep is not a private view that simply happens to be my own. In the intellectual history of the human race, this intuition has been formulated again and again. For us in the Western world, it has one of its most eloquent statements in some things that Plato, the father of philosophy, had to say in his later dialogues, or writings. Hence, I appeal to him for some confirmation of what I have written.

In two of his writings, the *Sophist* and the *Timaeus*, Plato made it clear that for him "the divine element in the world is to be conceived as a persuasive agency and not as a coercive agency." The words just quoted are Whitehead's summary of Plato's view. (I have used this summary by Whitehead for a reason that will appear later; but any reader of those dialogues will see the accuracy of the summary.) In earlier writings, too, but especially in the *Symposium* (which discusses love itself) and in the *Phaedrus* (which considers beauty), Plato approaches that final insight. Persuasion, for Plato, is lure, attraction, invitation, and solicitation, in contrast to force or the exercise of power. He urged that in the persuasive —tender, self-giving, receptive—aspects of human experience we have an intimation of the nature of the cosmic structure and the dynamic energy that moves through the universe. He rejected the more obvious and, on the surface, simpler notion that the world is a place where sheer coercion has absolute sway, just as he rejected the skeptical position that the world makes no sense at all and is merely a collection of things moving aimlessly, with neither purpose nor goal.

Plato was not a systematic philosopher, unlike his pupil

and critic Aristotle. He threw out hints, reported insight, concerned himself with a critical analysis of personal and social experience, and did not attempt a grandiose philosophical scheme. Doubtless, his intuition about persuasion does not always fit in with other ideas he expressed. What is significant for us is that in the latter part of a long life, spent not only in academic pursuits in the school he founded and directed but also in practical interests as an adviser to a Greek colonial ruler, he had come to feel strongly—and to express in poetic imagery—this conviction about persuasion or love. It was for him a theory, of course,—a profound speculation. That is to say, his conviction was built upon his thought and experience and then offered as the best explanation available of such meaning as he believed he had discovered in his own life—perhaps, above all, the meaning that he had learned that life could have when seen in light of the teaching, experience, and death of his beloved master Socrates, Athenian martyr to truth.

I have summarized Plato's intuition, which was the basis for his great theory, in the words of Whitehead. I have done this because Whitehead used those words in connection with the following: "Can there be any doubt that the power of Christianity lies in its *revelation in act*, of that which Plato divined in theory?" (These quotations, and the longer one which follows shortly, are from *Adventures of Ideas*, pp. 170-71; the italics are not in the original.) What did Whitehead mean by this? The explanation is found in his belief that what he called "the brief Galilean vision," in which Jesus of Nazareth was the central figure, was a concrete historical expression of the centrality of love in the cosmos. He wrote about "the appeal to the life of Christ as a revelation of the nature of God and of his agency [action] in the world." And then he went on to say: "The record is fragmentary, inconsistent, and uncertain. It is not necessary for me to express any opinion as to the proper reconstruction of the most likely tale of historical fact. . . . But there can be no doubt as to what elements in the record have evoked a response from all that is best in human nature. The Mother, the Child, and the bare manger; the lowly man, homeless and self-forgetful, with his message of peace, love, and sympathy; the suffering, the agony, the tender words as life ebbed, the final despair, and the whole with the authority of supreme victory."

Now Whitehead was a hardheaded thinker; he abhorred sentimentality and was very critical of conventional religious ideas. He had an enormous amount of common sense, which he did not lose when he wrote on philosophy. Educated as a mathematician at Trinity College, Cambridge, he lectured there in mathematics for many years before joining the faculty of the University of London as a professor of mathematical physics and a lecturer on the philosophy of science. He produced with Bertrand Russell, a great book on the principles of mathematics and logic. But he was also a humane man, sensitive to art, poetry, and fiction. His aesthetic sense led him to place the awareness of beauty (in the full meaning of the harmonious, which reconciles contrasts) at the heart of his thinking. When he went to Harvard University to end his days, first as a professor of philosophy and then in honored retirement, his intention was to work out a "vision of reality" that would take into account mathematics, physics, the other sciences, art, literature, moral awareness, and also religious feelings. For although Whitehead was not a "pious" person and had no use at all for what he styled the "vapid inanities" of much that goes by the name religion, he was convinced that this dimension in human experience is of supreme importance and that any view of things which omits it is bound to be truncated and hence inadequate to the facts.

Whitehead was prepared to go even farther and to insist that only in the context of persuasion or love can the belief in life's significance and in God have any intelligible meaning. He rejected utterly, and with indignation, ideas of God as a tyrannical ruler, or as an inert and "unmoved first cause," or as a changeless substance, or as a ruthless moralist. He knew that such ideas have been associated with the concept of God in Jewish and Christian teaching, and elsewhere as well. But he believed that such ideas contradict the insight about love or persuasion that Plato expressed but that were embodied vividly in the human life and achievement of the man of Nazareth. Whitehead was convinced that persuasion and tenderness—in fact, love—are basic and much more the truth about the world than power and force, however much appearances may seem to suggest the contrary. Thus, Whitehead was sure that if there is any sense in the concept of God it must be in terms of persuasion and tenderness, or love; and it must be recognized that only such love has the power to move the world and the men and women in it toward true satisfaction of potentiality and genuine wholeness.

What Whitehead said helps to make sense of that troublesome word God. For many people today the word suggests a dictator sitting on a heavenly throne and ordering things around in a tyrannical manner. This makes nonsense of human freedom and responsibility; and people rightly reject any such idea. Or, it means an unimaginable something or someone remote from the world, serving only as the logical explanation of how it happens that there is a world at all. This makes the concept irrelevant to human experience; such a God does not really count in human affairs or in the creation at large. Or people think the word refers to a moral governor who imposes from on high a set of laws that must be obeyed without question, with the penalty of damnation for disobedience, and for obedience the reward of a not very attractive heavenly existence after death. That seems an outrage to human moral sensitivity.

But God may be a word that points to something very different from any or all of these. It may point to a cosmic love "that will not let us go," a love so dynamic and inexhaustible that it continues for ever, providing what we have called the grain of the universe, and in itself greater than the love that any two or more human beings can ever know and express. It may indicate what we could call, following the analogy of the human lover, the "cosmic lover," or, in Dante's words, "the love that moves the sun and the other stars." If this should be the case, a very large part of conventional religious doctrine or theology would have to be rejected or undergo drastic and radical reconstruction. And that might not be a bad thing, especially since conventional doctrine has been so permeated by false notions of the meaning of the word God.

The fundamental question is whether such love, now seen as cosmic in its sweep, *is* the point of it all. Once the question has been phrased in that fashion, it presents itself to every man and woman. What will the answer be, once one has come to see the issues that are at stake? There is no way in which a positive answer—or a negative one, for that matter—can be forced upon anyone. If it were, it would not be one's own answer at all and therefore would not speak to one's own condition. Each of us can only speak for himself or herself—bear our own witness, positively or negatively. For my part, I am sure that a deep awareness of what it means to be human, in the way that in fact we *are* human and by the expression of that meaning in human loving, can lead to a positive answer. It does for me.

I should put it this way: If the meaning that we know in being human is found in the thrust toward self-fulfillment; if the way to this goal is through decisions made in association with and for the benefit of our fellows as well as for ourselves; if wholeness or integration emerges in the process of our becoming human, and if love known at the human level is the clue to the whole picture of human existence—if all this is true, then there must be something in the world that works that way too. After all is said and done, humanity is just as much part of the world as are sticks and stones and simians. It is not an alien intruder into the world from outside; it appears in it and comes from it and belongs to it. Whatever else it may be, human life is part of the total processive movement of nature. Should not this human experience of love—of giving-and-receiving, mutuality, tenderness, gentleness, willingness to risk, scorn of consequence in living in love's way—provide a clue to how things go? Granted that there is much that seems to point in the opposite direction: evil, wrong, imperfection, distortion, and the tragic twisting of life. Yet it is possible to make the daring and courageous claim that the positive aspect is ultimately dominant, and that love is greater than, and will triumph over, the negations of hate, evil, wrong, and distortion. Such a claim, with all its risks, can give validation and lasting worth to our experience of human loving. This is no conventional pietism but a readiness to live boldly. To use other words of Whitehead, this is no "rule of safety," but "an adventure of the spirit" (*Science and the Modern World*, p. 172).

And now I must venture to become very personal: this is the only way in which I can give some explanation of the deep conviction to which I have been brought during my lifetime.

I was brought up in a religiously minded family and I have every reason to know that my parents' beliefs were sincere if conventional. They were exemplary in church attendance and I always accompanied them. I was confirmed, of course, and became a regular communicant.

After completing my education, I tried two or three different kinds of work before I finally settled down to teaching. My academic interest had been in philosophy, specializing in what then—half a century ago—was usually called the philosophy of religion. Eventually I was ordained to the ministry and became an instructor and later a professor in this field in a large theological college. On occasion, I also taught part-time in a great university nearby. I wrote a number of books in my special field, some of which were said to be significant contributions to the subject.

But as the years went by and my reading and study continued, I found that I was not able to accept with any real conviction much of the conventional teaching with which I was familiar. Perhaps because by nature I was both inquiring and critical, I felt that much of what was said and taught around me could not stand up to serious examination. Often it seemed to lack adequate evidence; it was merely the expression of views that were accepted because they were part of a given position. In my teaching I did not have any particular occasion to reveal my doubts and questions, since my subject was related to wider philosophical issues in respect to religion and not necessarily to specific doctrinal positions. But in some of my more popular books I did indicate my attitude and got into trouble on one or two occasions with ecclesiastical authorities. Certainly many of my students were aware of the "radical" nature of my ideas. Of course, I continued to attend religious observances and take my full part in all that side of the college's life; but I realized that much of what went on often had very little personal meaning for me. Some people regarded me with suspicion as perhaps a "dangerous" person, but my teaching position was not seriously affected.

Then two things happened.

The first was the discovery that I was deeply loved by

another human being and that I could and did return that love. This was a personal revelation to me and no words are adequate to describe its wonder or to express my gratitude to the one who loved me and whom I loved. Here was something I could hold to, build on, and believe in. While the details of much conventional teaching were still unacceptable to me, the main emphasis or central affirmation began to make sense. Chief among religious beliefs was the faith that "God is love"; with it was the taking of such love as the criterion (along with the inevitable criterion of reasonable coherence) for all religious affirmations. This meant a complete revision of my ideas, including a total reconception of the basic religious structure.

The second thing was much more academic in its origin. Years before, I had heard Whitehead lecture and had been impressed by his personality but puzzled by his thought. I had read most of his books but they had not spoken directly to me. However, a few years before Whitehead's death in 1947, a friend who had just made a thorough study of these books said that in his judgment, "that man is the most important and rewarding thinker of our time." I decided to read him once again. And I discovered that he spoke to me as he had not done before. His general philosophical position commended itself to me and I accepted it as my own. But the *big* thing for me was his incidental and occasional comments on religion, some of which I have quoted in this book. His insistence on persuasion, tenderness, or love, as basic to the universe, and his stress on genuine religion as being concerned above all to relate men to that love, naturally fitted in with my own recent experience, gave it a setting in the world, and, along with the general Whiteheadian conception of an evolving, processive, interrelated, organic cosmos, opened to me the possibility of believing that this is indeed *how things go.*

161

I am sure that my own personal discovery of love, of loving and being loved, had prepared me for Whitehead's insight. Certainly I had come to know that my own process of becoming human, of making real my potentialities, and of achieving some measure of human wholeness, was entirely grounded in a love that was genuine, mutual, and enriching. I could not fail to think that somehow this experience had a basis in the structure of things and in the dynamic energy that works through things, whatever that structure and energy might be. Whitehead's general vision of reality and his specific emphasis on the "revelation in act of what Plato divined in theory" provided the rational support for all this. Words cannot be found to express my gratitude for the help I received from the writings of that great and good man.

So, I told myself, this *is* the point of it all. Things fell into place and I knew a peace of mind and spirit, which for years had been lacking in my life. This peace was not reached through any denial of anguish or suffering, but through acceptance of them as the price to be paid for the free gift of love. I was glad to take the risk of faith that love is the deepest and highest of truths. I could make my own the words of Dante. I could trust in "the love that moves the sun and the other stars" because it had been and still was love, the human reflection of cosmic love, that moved *me*.

I am not much worried about ecclesiastical institutions or the machinery of organized religion, although I realize that these are necessary for the social expression and communication of this trust in love because we are social creatures and need the strength and support of our fellows. Again, I am not bothered by what name people may wish to give to this thing that I believe so firmly. Not long ago someone said to me that I talked in a way which might be acceptable to a humanist. I could only reply that I was glad that this was so, provided the humanist would agree

---

162

that love does have cosmic quality and a cosmic thrust and hence may be spelled with an upper case "L" as well as with a lower case "l," appropriate to its referent in human experience. I added that I must also call myself a Christian because I found this conviction confirmed, vitalized, and made vividly compelling by the expression of love in a man who had loved, a man who had lived in Palestine two thousand years ago, and who was somehow still loose in the world to influence people like me.

What does it come to? For me, it comes to a deepening confidence, as very old age draws on, in the sheer worth of life. It comes to the feeling—but that word is far too weak to say what I intend—that those who love are sharers in a process that goes on through them and sometimes in spite of them, a drive to make love more available for more people in more places and in more ways and at more times. A month before his death, Whitehead said something about this, too, in what were probably his last carefully considered words. They were reported by his friend Lucien Price in his *Dialogues of Alfred North Whitehead* (p. 297): "Insofar as man partakes of [the creative process] does he partake of the divine, of God, and that participation is his immortality. . . . His true destiny as cocreator in the universe is his dignity and his grandeur."

To be a cocreator, to share however humbly in the dynamic thrust of the love "that makes the world go round," to find the ultimate meaning and final point of being human in just that chance to share: for me, this is the point of it all. That is meaning enough for this life and for any other there may be.